Start a Small Busine

Vera Hughes and
David Weller

Vera Hughes and David Weller jointly set up DEVA Training Services in 1980, working in a wide variety of organizations and businesses, and gaining experience of the different work practices and cultures of their very varied clients. At the same time, they were experiencing the joys and traumas of running their own small business, which lasted for some 25 years.

For the last 15 years they have reverted to their first love, the theatre, setting up another small business – Chester House Productions. They have written and staged ten very diverse presentations and have performed to over 27,000 people, in clubs and societies as well as in small festivals and arts centres, mainly across the south of England. Both their small businesses have thrived, so Vera and David are happy to pass on the fruits of their experience to you, the new entrepreneurs.

This book, their best-selling joint publication, now in its fourth edition and previously published as *Teach Yourself Set up a Successful Small Business*, has sold over 50,000 copies.

Start a Small Business

Vera Hughes and
David Weller

First published in Great Britain in 2010 by Hodder Headline. An Hachette UK company.

This revised and updated edition published 2015 by John Murray Learning

Previously published as *Set up a Successful Small Business*

Copyright © 2010, 2013, 2015 Vera Hughes and David Weller

British Library Cataloguing in Publication Data: a catalogue record for this title is available from the British Library.

ISBN: 978 1473 60918 1

eBook ISBN: 978 1473 60919 8

Cover image © Shutterstock.com

Typeset by Cenveo® Publisher Services.

Printed and bound in Grea⸺ ⸺⸺⸺⸺ by CPO ⸺⸺⸺⸺⸺ CR0 4YY.

John Murray Learning po⸺ and recyclable products a⸺ The logging and manufact⸺ environmental regulations⸺

Hodder & Stoughton Ltd
338 Euston Road
London NW1 3BH
www.hodder.co.uk

Acknowledgements

The authors gratefully acknowledge the help and expertise of
the following people: Tony Adams, Accountant, on all matters
to do with accounting; Baricz Eva for her Etsy story; Adrienne
Coles of Kuroi, for detailed advice on website design and
maintenance; Brenda Locke of Datacounts, on book-keeping
and Internet banking; Caroline Gilham of Carousel Cottage
Crafts, for her e-commerce experience; Charles Smith of CBS
Contracts, builder and decorator, on managing subcontractors;
Gillian Leach, Solicitor, on all matters to do with employing
others; and Larch Gauld, of Virtual Support Services, on
marketing through social networking.

Contents

The first step

In this chapter you will learn:

- ► *How to carry out some basic market research to see whether your business plan has a future*
- ► *How to research and deal with suppliers, including those based overseas*
- ► *How to set up a pilot scheme to check whether your business is viable*
- ► *How to assess your own suitability for setting up a small business.*

The first thing anyone needs before setting up any kind of business is an idea, or more precisely the idea of starting in business at all. Before the idea takes over too much, you need to ask yourself certain questions, which are:

▶ What precisely is the product or service I am going to offer?

▶ Why should customers buy my product or service rather than those that exist already?

The selling points

To help answer these questions, complete this questionnaire for your product or service.

Self-assessment: Identify your product and customers

1 What is your product or service?

2 What are its main selling points?

3 Who will your customers be?

4 What is their age range?

5 What is their income bracket?

6 Are they local, nationwide or worldwide (online selling)?

7 Who are your main competitors?

8 How well established are they?

9 Is it an expanding or contracting market?

10 How will your product or service differ?

When you have answered these questions as far as you can, your next step is to carry out some preliminary market research.

Market research

As a small trader or partnership, you cannot afford to embark on a very large market research exercise, but it is worthwhile trying to establish whether what sells well to friends and colleagues, or business contacts, will be bought by others.

You can research the market in an informal way by asking friends, family and colleagues what they think of your idea. A more business-like approach is to send out or give out a short questionnaire. You could do this at networking meetings, online, or with gatherings of family or friends. Expect a better response if you hand out the questionnaires personally and get people to complete them then and there.

Whichever method of distribution you choose, design your questionnaire carefully, taking these guidelines into account:

▶ Use one A4 sheet at most, or computer equivalent.

▶ Ask questions which require tick-box responses – people don't like to write long answers.

▶ If you ask people to rate an attribute of your product/service, give them an even number of boxes to tick – four or six. If you give them five they are likely to go down the middle.

▶ Leave space for additional comments.

▶ Don't ask for a lot of personal information – you might be infringing the Data Protection Act.

▶ Make giving their name optional – people often give 'truer' answers if they know they are anonymous.

▶ Draw up a good system for analysing the responses.

Figure 1.1 is an example of a questionnaire James might send out. He is thinking of setting up a garden design and landscaping business in and around his local villages.

JAY'S GARDENS

Please complete this short questionnaire by ticking the appropriate boxes; feel free to add any comments you may wish to make.

1 Are you considering enhancing all or part of your garden within the next two years?

YES   NO

2 If yes, would you consider employing a professional to help you with (tick as many as are appropriate):

design ☐

planting ☐

hard landscaping ☐

maintenance ☐

3 Please rate the importance to you of the following by ticking the appropriate column.

Subject	Very important	Important	Somewhat important	Not important
Reliability				
Creativity				
Competitive pricing				
Ease of maintenance				

4 How far away do you live from the address below?

Within 5 miles ☐

Within 10 miles ☐

Within 20 miles ☐

Over 20 miles ☐

5 Please write any further comments you would like to make:

_____

_____

_____

Optional:

Your name:_____

Your contact details:_____

Please return this questionnaire to: James Gardner, Jay's Gardens, (address)

Thank you for completing this questionnaire.

Figure 1.1 Example marketing questionnaire

If James gets a 90 per cent 'no' to Question 1, he can be pretty sure that either his local market is saturated, or he has asked the wrong people, or all his local gardens are perfect! If he has a favourable response to his first question, the other responses will give him some idea of which parts of his service potential clients will find the most valuable.

Try it now: Design your own questionnaire

Now design your own questionnaire, decide on its distribution method and devise a system (computer- or paper-based) for analysing the responses.

Remember this: Seek advice on getting started

For help and impartial advice, contact your local council, which often has good systems for helping small businesses to get started. Your local Business Link and many other organizations can help you think through your idea, set targets and begin to get your business off the ground. See Chapter 12 for useful website addresses.

Your suppliers

Every business needs suppliers of some sort, even if they are only for office stationery. This time you are the customer, and will need your supplies to be reliable, well made and reasonably priced, with a good delivery service.

If you have been working in a bigger business and have decided to go it alone, or if you are converting a hobby into a business, you are probably aware of good sources of supply already. However, if you need additional, perhaps specialist, parts, equipment or stock, or items unfamiliar to you, you need to do some serious research.

Start by asking colleagues or other small business proprietors in your line of business where they get their supplies. They will probably be happy to share this information with you. You can look in publications such as the *Yellow Pages* or *Thomson Local*, but trade catalogues are usually much more informative and the Internet is an excellent source of information.

When you place an order in the UK, you know that you must be precise in what you are ordering and where it should be delivered. You also have to take into account delivery times, carriage charges and discounts. If you order from outside the UK, you will be stepping into the import business.

ORDERING FROM ABROAD

To import sounds more daunting than it actually is. You are merely buying from an overseas supplier instead of a home supplier, and the difference is all to do with procedures, currency and time – things which can be calculated or learned. We deal here with the mechanics of getting the goods from overseas to your place of work, not with choosing suppliers and negotiating deals.

▶ Placing an order

Before you place your order you should get a **firm quotation** from your supplier. Be very specific about what you want on the quotation; this is best done by a formal request for a quotation, setting out:

- ▶ who you are and what your business is
- ▶ who your bankers are, to help establish your creditworthiness
- ▶ the goods or services you want, and how they are to be packed and marked
- ▶ possible questions
- ▶ delivery dates and terms
- ▶ what insurance arrangements you intend to use.

Once you have a firm quotation, you can place your order. You can order by phone, fax or email, but the order should be confirmed in writing on your headed paper. Remember to agree with your supplier:

- ▶ quantity, description and price
- ▶ method of despatch (air, sea or land)
- ▶ method of delivery (post, courier, etc.) and delivery destination (port, warehouse, etc.)

- delivery times, which are likely to be longer, but not necessarily
- the point at which the insurance by the supplier stops and the insurance by you begins (see insurance later in this chapter)
- whether the prices quoted include insurance
- carriage charges
- discounts
- method of payment.

If you are doing regular business with a supplier, it may be beneficial to set up a trading agreement and account.

When considering quotations and pricing, take into account that currency values fluctuate, so you need to be sure which currency you are dealing in and in which currency the price is fixed. For large orders, buyers can secure the price well in advance of delivery by taking a 'position' or 'option' on the currency value with the bank. This needs some knowledge and experience of currency markets and values.

In EU countries, if you are using suppliers and you are VAT-registered, you may not have to pay VAT on the goods you purchase. In any case, if you pay VAT, it will be at the UK rate, not at the rate of the supplying country.

▶ Documentation

These are the most common items of documentation:

- **Advice note** On receipt of your order, the supplier should confirm to you all the details mentioned above, including date of expected despatch and length of delivery time.
- **Bill of lading** This is the receipt given by a ship's master to the supplier of the goods, stating in detail the goods loaded on board the ship. The bill of lading is an important part of the papers which travel with goods being imported or exported.
- **Air waybill** This is a sort of aviation bill of lading. It is a contract of carriage when goods are sent by air, and acts as a receipt for the goods. It is made out by the airline.

- ▶ **Delivery note** A detailed description, for the supplier, of the actual goods in that delivery.

- ▶ **Carriage note** Details, from a transport company, of the number of crates, boxes or pallets.

- ▶ **Pro forma invoice** You will also receive a pro forma invoice, probably stating the preferred method of payment.

For details of customs and other documents, seek advice from your clearing agent.

▶ Customs and transportation

If you are intending to import fairly large quantities of goods, it could be wise, to start with, to use a clearing agent, who will deal with all the customs and transport side of it for you. Seek advice from your local Chamber of Commerce.

If you are importing on a very small or limited basis, the Post Office is an excellent transporter of goods. Your supplier will complete all the customs documentation necessary. If the order is a sample, and not for onward sale by you, ask the supplier to mark the goods 'Sample only – of no commercial value'. This should mean that you do not have to pay customs duty.

You will probably have to collect your packages from the sorting office, and pay any VAT and duty due at that point. You will probably have to pay a Post Office clearance fee. Keep the Post Office label on the package, as this will constitute your VAT receipt for book-keeping purposes.

▶ Payment

Bear in mind that some overseas suppliers may require payment up front because you have little or no trading history. They will usually require this to be done through a **bank transfer**, which will incur bank charges for you. Some suppliers will not accept orders below a minimum amount.

You may also be asked for **trade references**, which can be difficult for new enterprises.

As in the UK, damaged items must be reported immediately to the supplier, who will usually issue a **credit note** against subsequent orders.

The main methods of payment are:

1 **Cash** Sent by registered post, this is popular in less developed countries for small orders.

2 **Via the bank** The most normal way of paying your suppliers is by bank transfer. Send a letter of authorization to your bank, detailing account numbers and accounts.

3 **Via the Post Office** An international payment coupon (rather like a postal order) can be bought at your local post office and sent by post to the supplier. It is suitable for small amounts.

▶ Insurance

You need to be sure that your goods are insured until they reach your doorstep. These are the most common terms used when despatching goods:

▶ **FOB – Free on Board** The price quoted includes everything until the goods are loaded on to the ship or plane. This does not include insurance.

▶ **CIF – Cost Insurance Freight** This means that everything is covered, including insurance, up to delivery at your warehouse except the cost of transport from the port or airport in the UK. You will have to arrange and pay for the cost of transport, but the goods remain insured.

▶ **C & F – Cost and Freight** This means that the goods are not insured, so you will have to make your own insurance arrangements.

As you can see, it is important that you are clear about the terms under which your goods will be supplied, so make sure they appear on the quotation you have requested.

Importing small quantities of goods is quite easy, particularly if you use the postal services. Importing large quantities is obviously more complicated. Seek all the advice you can before you start. Importing from EU countries should be a simpler matter.

RESEARCHING YOUR SUPPLIERS

Before doing this research you need to know what you want, so draw up your product or service specifications. If you are opening a shop, for example, as well as stock in the appropriate range, colours and so on, you will need wrapping or packing materials, cleaning products, office stationery, price tags or shelf edging tickets, etc. If you decide to sell jewellery on a network marketing basis, as well as stock you would need display cloths, order forms and, again, wrapping materials. A craft-based enterprise might need supplies of wood, metal, glass, fabric or other materials. A small manufacturing business needs the raw materials to make its own component parts, or to buy those parts in from suppliers.

Whatever your business, another list is very helpful here. You could construct a table something like the one Samantha, who is opening a fashion boutique called Affordable Fashion, has decided to use. A spreadsheet would be very useful for this, but it can be done on paper:

Affordable Fashion Suppliers

Suits Skirts Tops Dresses Trousers

Supplier 1

Prices
Delivery schedule
Settlement terms
Product quality

Supplier 2

Prices
Delivery schedule
Settlement terms
Product quality

Supplier 3

Prices
Delivery schedule
Settlement terms
Product quality
etc.

Search out more than one supplier, if possible, to compare the service they are offering and to have an alternative supplier if you need one, perhaps in an emergency.

All these supplies are for the ongoing running of the business, not the start-up requirements, which you can study in the next chapter.

> **Try it now: Research your suppliers**
>
> Whatever your business, make a list of all the suppliers you will need. Research two or three suppliers for each and draw up a chart which you can fill in as you receive this information. Use Samantha's 'Affordable Fashion' Suppliers' chart as an example.

Pilot scheme

For some businesses it is possible to try out your business on a small scale to see what works and what does not. James, who is planning to start a garden design and landscaping consultancy, for example, could take on work in the evenings and at weekends, charging only for materials, while still managing the local garden centre. This would give him a good idea of what his potential customers really want, how much they are prepared to pay and the suppliers and/or subcontractors he would need to engage.

Perhaps you are expanding a hobby into a business; many craft-based enterprises start in this way. You will already know your suppliers, but who, exactly, will be your customers and what are they prepared to pay? Take a stand at a small craft fair and see what sells.

Many small businesses, such as plumbers, electricians, and painters and decorators have done a lot of DIY and then started helping the neighbours. Maybe now is the time to put the enterprise on a more business-like footing, work for any necessary qualifications and ask people who know your work to recommend you to others, on a commercial basis. For people who work in other people's homes, it is important to gain experience of dealing with many different types of customer before giving up the day job.

If you have invented something or made something you are convinced will sell, it is essential to try it out as a pilot scheme before launching your product to the general public. Perhaps you have developed a new kitchen gadget, or designed some special clothes for babies with eczema. Have a small batch made, let the end users use the items for a reasonable length of time and monitor how they get on.

For certain businesses, such as retail or taking on a franchise, it is difficult to run a pilot scheme. You either open a shop or you don't. However, you could buy a small amount of stock and try it out on friends and neighbours, including people you do not know well – they are likely to give you objective opinions.

If you are thinking of opening a coffee shop, a café or a restaurant, running a pilot scheme is even more difficult. It is unlikely that you will embark on this type of enterprise without some experience yourself, or at least with a partner who knows what he or she is doing. In these circumstances, good planning and market research are essential.

Try it now: Develop a pilot scheme

Consider whether you can run a pilot scheme or not. Make a plan to test your product or service, put the plan into action, collect feedback and adjust as necessary. There seems to be so much planning and trying out before you can really get your business up and running, but all this preparation really does pay off.

Here are some guidelines to help you plan your pilot scheme:

For a service
* Who will you target?
* How are you going to make contact?
* What, exactly, will you be offering?
* What are you going to charge?
* How are you going to know what works and what does not?

It's helpful to keep a log of what you did and for whom, and what worked well and what didn't. Write up these notes as soon as you have finished the job.

For a product

* Get a small batch made up – how many?
* Or buy in a small batch – how many?
* Is there a range of colours and styles?
* If so, which will you try out?
* Who will you target as guinea pigs?
* How will you make contact?
* How long will you want them to try the product?
* How will you get feedback? Leave a card/questionnaire for them to complete? Watch them use the product? Test the product after it has been used?

Only you will know how to run your pilot scheme. If it works, fine; you can go on from there. If it does not, even after feedback and adjustments, at least you know what the situation is and have not wasted too much time, energy and money in launching a business which is going to fail.

Remember this: Have faith in your product or service

If you, yourself, do not have absolute faith in your product or the quality of your service, you will never get your business off the ground. Do not be put off if other people's reactions do not initially match your enthusiasm; but at the same time be prepared to adjust your ideas after objective feedback.

Your personal attributes

You may have a good, sound product or service to sell, but what about your own attributes? Are you the sort of person who can make a go of your own small business?

Self-assessment: Assess your attributes

This exercise comes in five parts. After reading the guidelines at the beginning of each part, assess yourself by rating your abilities. If you find you have a few low scores you will know the areas you must work on personally. If you end up with low scores over all, perhaps running your own business is not for you.

Part 1: Motivation

The belief in your product or service is the first step in self-motivation; what follows depends on your own ability to move off the starting line and keep up the momentum.

Sometimes people feel that those who have their own businesses are lucky, because they can suit themselves whether they work or not. To a certain extent this is true, of course: if you decide one morning that you would rather stay in bed than turn out in the cold to sell your product or service, that is up to you – your competitors will be delighted!

Self-motivation is an attitude of mind as much as anything, and your attitude must at all times be to develop your business. If you are a sole trader, this can be more difficult, since you may not have anyone else to help you with your motivational process. So self-motivation should perhaps be coupled with self-discipline. Determine to set yourself a regular business routine, and do all you can to keep to it. As you achieve this regular routine, you will find that your self-motivation improves dramatically. There is nothing like a successful meeting or telephone call to stimulate motivation – the hard work is the initial effort needed to arrange that meeting or make that telephone call in the first place.

Rate yourself on a score of 1–4, where 1 is poor and 4 is excellent.

Statement	Rating
1 I can stick to a self-imposed business routine.	☐
2 I am good at making contact with people.	☐
3 I can be flexible in my working day.	☐
4 I have someone to talk matters over with.	☐

5 I can do the boring tasks as well as the exciting ones. ☐

6 I believe my product/service is wonderful. ☐

Total out of 24 _____

Any weaknesses? Then you know what to work on.

If you have a score of 3 or under on the last question, you are probably not ready to set up your own business.

Part 2: Organizational ability

An absolute requirement of anyone who starts a new business is the ability to operate in an organized way. You cannot work effectively in a muddle.

This has nothing to do with the workshop with wood shavings on the floor, or even the desk with papers strewn over it. This is the ability to know when and where the next appointment is, of dealing with correspondence quickly and efficiently, of being able to put your hand on specific pieces of information promptly and responding to queries or enquiries.

Statement	Rating
1 I always arrive in good time.	☐
2 I answer emails/letters within 48 hours.	☐
3 I respond to voicemail messages within 24 hours.	☐
4 I can set up a system for retrieving email and voicemail messages.	☐
5 My email filing system is in good order.	☐
6 My paper filing system is in good order.	☐
7 I arrive at meetings with the right paperwork.	☐
8 My car tax disk is never out of date.	☐
9 My diary/diaries are always up to date.	☐

Total out of 36 _____

Again you will have highlighted, or rather lowlighted, the points you need to work on. If you are a very disorganized person, you may need to employ someone on a part-time basis to keep you on track, so take this into account when considering your start-up requirements in the next chapter.

Part 3: Management of time

Whether you are the chairperson of an international business organization or a sole trader, the amount of time available to you is exactly the same: there are precisely 24 hours in the day for both parties.

How those 24 hours are utilized is where the differences arise. Chairs of multinationals probably have other people around them to ease the pressure on their time, while the sole trader more than likely has no such luxury, or at best has very limited help.

The management of available time effectively is therefore significant, requiring, once again, a high degree of self-discipline.

One of the greatest causes of mismanagement of time is the very human one of doing those things which we want to do. You can always find a valid reason for putting off the unpleasant job.

These are some top time-management tips:

✳ **Plan**
  ▷ Use a to-do list: you may need a long-term list and a daily list. Write down every item and cross it out when it is done.
  ▷ Use a booklet or your desktop or laptop. Don't keep it in your head.
✳ **Prioritize**
  ▷ Categorize your tasks into A, top priority, through to D, low priority.
  ▷ Do the A list first, particularly if they are the unpleasant tasks, rather than those easy Ds.
  ▷ Read important communications first; set the others aside for reading later.
✳ **Control your telephone calls.**
  If you are *making the call*:
  ▷ plan to make calls in batches
  ▷ have all the information to hand
  ▷ quickly get to the purpose of the call
  ▷ when the business is finished, summarize what you have agreed, thank the person you have been calling and end the call.
  ▷ If you are *receiving the call*:
  ▷ make notes of what the caller wants
  ▷ arrange a specific call-back time, if necessary
  ▷ keep asking questions until you get the call-back name and number right.

* **Control your emails**
  ▷ Organize your system to 'spam out' the junk emails.
  ▷ Read emails in batches (not as soon as they arrive).
  ▷ Respond to the top-priority emails first.
* **Exercise self-discipline**
  ▷ Get it right first time, whatever 'it' is.
  ▷ Avoid procrastination – get on with it.
  ▷ Do one thing at a time.
  ▷ Say 'no' if you have to.
* **Travel productively**
  ▷ Plan your route carefully (can you rely on your satnav?).
  ▷ Use car time to learn from CDs.
  ▷ Use train time to read, write and plan.
  ▷ Use waiting time to make phone calls.

Rate yourself on your time management: 1 is poor, 4 is excellent.

Statement	Rating
1 I do top-priority tasks first.	☐
2 I make phone calls in batches.	☐
3 I always ring back when I've promised to do so.	☐
4 I can end calls courteously and promptly.	☐
5 My system can 'spam out' unwanted emails.	☐
6 I read emails in batches, not as and when.	☐
7 I do one task at a time.	☐
8 I can say 'no' if necessary.	☐
9 I use car time productively.	☐
10 I use train time productively.	☐
11 I use waiting time productively.	☐
12 I always know where I'm going.	☐
Total out of 48	————

Part 4: Energy and health

To run a small business well you need a lot of energy and good health – you literally cannot afford to be ill. The business depends on you, often on you alone. The following rating exercise is not based on medical criteria, but on experience of what you need to do to maintain your energy and your good health. For example, it is wise to have a regular, probably annual, check-up at a well man or well woman clinic so that any potential problems are detected early and you can plan how to deal with them.

Rate yourself on your energy and health: 1 is poor, 4 is excellent.

Statement	Rating
1 I am generally healthy.	☐
2 If/when I have a health problem, I know how to manage it.	☐
3 If I begin to fall ill, I do something about it.	☐
4 Generally I sleep well.	☐
5 I will arrange to take some holiday each year.	☐
6 I will arrange to attend a well man or well woman clinic regularly.	☐
7 Generally I have plenty of energy.	☐

Total out of 28 _____

Very few people can be on top form all the time. Running a business is a physical and mental strain, as well as being exciting and pleasurable. Recognize this and manage your health accordingly.

Part 5: Communication skills

You will need good communication skills, whatever your business, but the degree of skill varies according to the business you are setting up. If your work is mainly computer-based, if you are a website designer for example, you will still need to be able to communicate with your clients to find out what they really want. It may be that someone else actually writes the copy for the website, so your written communication skills may not be quite so important.

If your business involves selling in any way, your interpersonal communication skills will obviously be of the highest importance, but you will still need to be able to communicate in writing to a certain extent.

Consultants often have to write proposals, which need to be carefully constructed and well written. Their verbal skills should be equally good, as they are often working with small groups or on a one-to-one basis.

How good are you on the telephone? Record one of your telephone conversations if you can (and also listen to your own voicemail message), having let the person on the other end know that you are recording (but only your end – their end will not be heard). When listening to the recording afterwards, do not think in general terms of how good and bad it is, but analyse whether:

* all the words can be clearly heard
* you say a lot of ums and ers
* you repeat yourself too much
* your voice sounds pleasant and friendly (try smiling down the phone).

The final part of this exercise is for you to assess how good your communication skills are. You might have enough courage to ask someone else to complete this assessment, where 1 is poor and 4 is excellent.

Statement	Rating
1 I talk easily.	☐
2 I listen well.	☐
3 I can explain myself clearly.	☐
4 I can understand what others are trying to say.	☐
5 My telephone manner is pleasant and friendly.	☐
6 I speak fluently on the phone.	☐
7 My text messages are understandable.	☐
8 My spelling, grammar and punctuation are good.	☐
9 My written communication is well constructed.	☐
10 I can write good, plain, correct, understandable English.	☐

Total out of 40 _____

It might be interesting now to add the five different totals together to get an overall picture of your personal attributes. This table will help you:

Assessment	Total
1 Part 1: Motivation	☐
2 Part 2: Organizational ability	☐
3 Part 3: Management of time	☐
4 Part 4: Energy and health	☐
5 Part 5: Communication skills	☐

Total out of 176 _____

You have already analysed your weaker points in each part, so now look at the grand total and try to determine what it tells you. Are you ready to set up your own business? This is not a scientifically proven assessment, but you could draw the following conclusions:

✳ If you scored roughly in the top one-third, between 120 and 176, you are probably well on the way to having the attributes you need.

✳ If you scored between 50 and 120, there is a lot of work to do.

✳ If you scored below 50, have a good look at all your weak points to see if there is anything you can do to improve the score. If the outlook is too daunting, perhaps you are personally not yet ready to set up your own business.

Remember this: Find a business 'buddy'

If you are a sole trader, it can be difficult to find someone to talk matters over with; someone outside your immediate family to be your mentor or 'buddy' might be a good idea. Perhaps arrange regular meetings where you can buy them a drink and bounce ideas off them.

Try it now: Buy a petty cash book

Go out and buy yourself a petty cash book. Start recording, week by week, every small item you spend on your potential business, because you can often claim this in retrospect, after the official start date. Keep all receipts (taxi fares, stationery purchases, including the petty cash book, car park tickets and so on). Ask yourself: 'Am I doing this for business reasons only?' If the answer is 'yes', you can probably claim it as a genuine business expense.

Focus point

You have listed the selling points of your product or service, done some preliminary market research, listed your suppliers, run a pilot scheme where possible and assessed your personal attributes. Have you also bought a petty cash book?

Next step

If all these steps have turned out well, or at least satisfactorily, you can really begin to get your business off the ground. Chapter 2 is about starting up, considering your method of trading, your business plan, business finance and whether you will be working at home, from home or in rented premises. So get going and good luck!

Starting up

In this chapter you will learn:

▶ *About the different forms your company might take – sole trader, partnership, limited company, limited partnership or charity – and which one will best suit you*

▶ *How to draw up a business plan*

▶ *How to price your products or services*

▶ *About various possible sources of start-up capital*

▶ *How to approach banks when seeking a business loan*

▶ *About the various options for your business premises – will your business be based in your home or in a factory or office?*

Now your business idea is firmly taking root. You have defined what your business is, where it fits into the market and you have done some preliminary research. You have satisfied yourself that self-employment is for you and perhaps have been able to run a small pilot scheme. So you are ready to start up.

Where should you start? It is important to put your business on a business-like footing, and there are many things to think about and set in motion, seemingly all at once.

Self-assessment: Basic decisions

Answer these questions to help you to analyse what decisions you need to make fairly early on.

1 Will you set up as a sole trader?

2 Or will you be in a partnership or a limited partnership?

3 What is the main difference between a sole trader or a partnership and a limited company?

4 Why should you make a business plan and what should it include?

5 How much will you charge for your product or service?

6 What is the difference between mark-up and margin?

7 Will you need start-up capital?

8 Where will you go to obtain this finance?

9 Where will you be based – at home, in an office or a shop, etc.?

10 What do you need to decide to get your premises up and running?

Methods of trading

Are you going to be a sole proprietor or a partner? Are you going to set up a limited company, or a limited partnership? Will you, perhaps, buy into a franchise? You might even become a registered charity. Look at each of these options, and decide which is appropriate for your business. You will need to have certain details on your stationery and what you decide will have a great bearing on your tax returns.

SOLE TRADER OR SOLE PROPRIETOR

If you are a one-person business, perhaps working from home, probably the best method of trading is as a sole trader. You do not need to register with any official body, but you do need some stationery with your name and business address. You should also have a document displayed in your office showing the name and address of your business and its proprietor(s). You need to inform HM Revenue & Customs (HMRC) and the Department of Work and Pensions (DWP) that you are self-employed and, if your turnover (that is, the amount of money you actually take in sales in a financial year) is £81,000 or more (2014/15 figures), you need to be VAT-registered. This figure may change each year. It is surprising how quickly your turnover will reach this figure.

If you are trading under your own name – for instance 'John Robinson Associates', or 'J. Robinson' or something very similar – you do not need to check whether someone else is trading under the same name. If you choose to trade under a name which is quite different from yours (for example, 'Parisian Photos'), check with your solicitor that there are no legal objections to your doing so. Your own name and address must still appear on your stationery.

As a sole trader, you are personally responsible for all your business transactions. This means that your personal income, from whatever source, your house, your car and even your estate after your death can be used to pay off debts. Some people make sure that the house is at least in joint names and that other possessions (such as the car) are registered in the name of another member of the family. Check with your solicitor the best way of covering yourself. You do not have to have your accounts audited, but it is as well to employ an accountant who specializes in very small businesses to prepare your annual accounts and tax returns for HMRC purposes.

PARTNERSHIP

If two or more of you are working together in the business, you can trade as a partnership. Like a sole trader, you do not have to register your business, but you do have to:

- show your names and address on your stationery
- inform HMRC and the DWP that you are self-employed
- check that any name under which you choose to trade is legally acceptable
- register for VAT if your turnover exceeds £81,000 per year (2014/15 figures).

All the partners are collectively and individually liable for the debts of the business. This includes any business debts of any of the partners, even if you do not know that these debts have been incurred.

You are not required by law to draw up a **partnership agreement,** but it is wise to do this, setting out all the conditions under which you have agreed to enter into business together. A solicitor specializing in small businesses and partnerships will be able to advise you.

The partnership ceases instantly upon the death of any of the partners, so it is wise to take out life insurance on each partner so that the remaining partner(s) have enough money to continue trading if they want to. The deceased partner's share of the business becomes part of his or her personal estate.

As with a sole trader, you do not have to have your accounts audited, but it is wise to employ an accountant for HMRC purposes.

A word of warning: Partnerships often do not last, because the partners fall out, mostly over finance or the contribution each makes to the business. A husband-and-wife partnership can be particularly difficult. You need to learn to work together as well as living together, which can put quite a strain on the marriage and the family. A husband-and-wife team often opt to trade as a limited company, or a limited partnership so that their liability is limited to their business pursuits.

LIMITED COMPANY

Many small businesses choose to set themselves up as a limited company. The big advantage of this method of trading is that your business liability is limited to the business, and you would not be required to pay debts out of your personal moneys, except in the case of fraud.

A limited company may have one shareholder only who could act as a director and company secretary, and the company must be registered with the **Companies Registration Office** (CRO) at Companies House, Crown Way, Maindy, Cardiff CF14 3UZ. Telephone its Contacts Centre on 0303 1234 500 or visit its website – www.companieshouse.gov.uk

The company's letters and emails must show its name, address, place of registration ('England', 'England and Wales' or 'Scotland') and the registration number. The fact that it is 'limited' must appear somewhere on the paper – either in the company name or as a separate statement. The stationery must also show the names (first name or initials plus surname) of either all the directors or none of them.

Companies House are beginning to take a tough line with companies that don't comply with these legal requirements. It is a criminal offence not to follow these rules on your company's letters and emails! On conviction, any guilty director or company faces a penalty of up to £1,000. If the stationery is not corrected, you could face a further fine of up to £100 per day. These rules don't apply to other forms of company stationery such as invoices which require just the company's registered name. If in doubt, check with Companies House.

The accounts must be properly audited by a registered auditor within ten months of the end of the company's financial year and filed annually at the CRO, so that anyone, particularly shareholders who are not directors of the company, can inspect them if they wish. The accountant is usually appointed at the first annual general meeting and continues as auditor as long as both parties wish.

Very small companies may not have to file annual accounts because of the Totally Exempt Companies System. Ask your accountant's advice.

You raise capital by selling shares in the company to the directors and others. The chair of the company, if one is appointed, is normally responsible to the shareholders.

The outline of the company's trading purposes and methods is drawn up in the **Memorandum and Articles of Association** (often known as 'Mem and Arts'). The Memorandum outlines the purpose of the company (its overall strategy) and the Articles of Association outline the way in which it will work – number of directors, voting rights and so on – (the company tactics). These documents need to be drawn up carefully; you should employ a solicitor.

You can buy a ready-made limited company 'off-the-shelf' from a company registration agent, with its Mem and Arts already prepared; virtually all you need to do is fill in the names of the director(s) and secretary and the company's proposed address, and pay the appropriate fee. You need to be sure that any such business meets your own requirements.

You can, of course, buy a business which already exists, including its goodwill, so that you can start trading straight away. In this case you need to look very carefully at its accounts, because they can be deceptive (without any intention to deceive). Employ an accountant for this: it is a false economy not to do so.

Try it now: Find an accountant and/or solicitor

This chapter refers frequently to your accountant and solicitor. A good accountant, one who specializes in small businesses, is particularly helpful at this stage. Do some preliminary research on who your accountant and solicitor should be. See Chapter 12 for information on what they can do for you.

LIMITED PARTNERSHIP

A limited partnership (LLP) combines the flexibility and status of a partnership with limited liability for its members. The potential liability of a member is limited to the amount that the member has agreed to contribute to the partnership if the LLP goes into liquidation.

The LLP is required to submit annual accounts to Companies House, and if necessary have them audited by a qualified accountant, unless Small Business Exemption applies; ask your accountant about this. Companies House must also be notified of any changes in partners and particulars, just as if the LLP were a limited company.

FRANCHISE

This has become a very popular way of starting up in business, and can be a sensible way of doing so because you can profit from the know-how of the franchisor (you would be the franchisee). Some very well-known companies run a franchise – household names like Cartridge World, Green Thumb UK, Kall Kwick, Prontaprint and Wimpy, to name a few. Opportunities are available in at least 30 different industry sectors. The *Franchise World Directory* gives details of all available franchise businesses.

The **advantages** of becoming a franchisee are:

▶ You are trading under a well-known name.

▶ You receive initial and ongoing advice and training in, for example, merchandising, stock control, buying, employing staff, book-keeping, etc.

▶ Franchisors often have a special arrangement with a bank and/or key suppliers for getting start-up money, which can reduce the burden of franchise fees.

▶ You are part of nationwide advertising.

▶ Sometimes the franchisor will find suitable premises and will lease or mortgage the premises to the franchisee.

The **disadvantages** are:

▶ You have to pay a franchise fee.

▶ You would have to pay an ongoing management fee – probably between 5 and 7 per cent of the turnover.

▶ The start-up capital can be quite large – up to £500,000 – but can be as low as £5,000. However, depending on your credit rating and the standing of the franchisor, banks could advance up to 50–60 per cent.

▶ In most networks you have to stick strictly to the systems laid down by the franchisor, so freedom to trade in the manner in which you wish to trade can be limited.

There are two main types of franchise for the small business:

1 Retailing in a wide variety of fashion shops and eating establishments: income depends on the profits made.

2 Rendering a service, such as carpet cleaning or car tuning: income often depends on the number of hours worked.

The British Franchise Association (telephone 01491 578050) is also a good source of information. Its website address is www.thebfa.org.uk

REGISTERED CHARITY

Tax advantages are likely to be available to a charity: generally most charities are exempt from income tax, corporation tax and capital gains tax. A charity which wishes to reclaim tax will need to register with HMRC Charities. Some supplies to charities are specifically exempted from VAT.

HMRC Charities gives information about tax relief and tax obligations (including VAT) at www.hmrc.gov.uk/charities/index.htm on issues such as trading, fund-raising, stamp duty and giving to charities. You can also make enquiries by telephone, email or post. See the website for current contact details.

To qualify as a charity, an organization will have to be for charitable purposes only and be for the public benefit. This applies to England and Wales; the law in Scotland and Northern Ireland is different. It is a complicated matter to register as a charity, so seek advice from a solicitor who specializes in this area of work.

MULTI-LEVEL MARKETING

This is a very specialized method of trading sometimes called 'network marketing'. Multi-level marketing is not illegal, and can make quite substantial income for those who wish to employ this trading method. It is a respectable development of pyramid selling, which got itself a bad name in the 1960s.

Multi-level marketing works in the following way. You join a trading scheme as a 'participant' and buy goods or services from the person or people running the scheme, or from other participants. You then sell these goods or services to the general public in their homes.

You make a profit on the difference between the cost (buying) price and the selling price and usually other rewards such as:

▶ bonuses for recruiting new participants

▶ commission on sales of your products made by other participants

▶ higher bonuses or commission if you are promoted to a higher level in the scheme

▶ payments for providing services (e.g. training) to other participants.

You need to be good at selling things and/or recruiting other participants if you are to make a substantial income from this type of scheme.

There are very strict rules for multi-level marketing companies. Visit the Department for Business, Innovation and Skills website at www.bis.gov.uk.

Multi-level marketing can be a profitable way of doing business, but you need to beware of illegal schemes, or getting caught up in a legal scheme without fully realizing its implications.

Try it now: Four steps to setting up your small business

✳ **Step 1:** Use the previous pages to decide which method of trading is best for you. Consult your accountant and/or solicitor as necessary.

✳ **Step 2:** Take any necessary steps to register your business.

✳ **Step 3:** Inform HM Revenue & Customs of your change of status.

✳ **Step 4:** Design your stationery accordingly.

Your business plan

If you are going to apply for a loan or a grant for your business, a business plan is essential. Even if you do not need start-up finance (perhaps yours is a consultancy or a 'home' service where you are working from your own home and visiting other people), a business plan helps you face the future in a realistic way. It is very important to do this if you are working with one or two other people, so that each of you agrees, and knows, where you are heading.

WRITE YOUR BUSINESS PLAN

This is important, particularly if you are applying for start-up finance.

▶ **Step 1**

Visit your local banks, and building societies that have become banks, and ask for a starter pack for setting up a small business. They are all different and all helpful in their own way. Building societies which are still 'mutual' are not usually as geared up for businesses.

▶ **Step 2**

Write your business plan. Use the starter packs as a guideline or choose which one is the most comprehensive and write down what your plans are. Use the headings below to guide your thoughts.

(NAME OF YOUR BUSINESS)
BUSINESS PLAN

The purpose of your business

What are you selling and who will your customers or clients be? You have already thought about this in Chapter 1. Are you a retailer, rendering a service, creating artefacts, manufacturing products, opening an eating establishment? What, exactly?

The competition

Where you fit in and where you differ. Again, you will already have established this in Chapter 1. What makes your business special?

Your method of trading

You now know which method of trading is best for you, but a business plan is often for other people to look at, particularly if you are seeking finance, so write down your chosen method of trading and the rationale behind your choice.

Your marketing strategy

How are you going to let people know that you have arrived? Which of these best suits your business? It may be a mixture of several marketing 'tools'.

- ▶ *Mailshots*: Good for consultancies and business to business

- ▶ *Leaflets and flyers*: For very small 'home' services and any business where you go to other people

- ▶ *Website*: Essential if you are selling 'online' (e-commerce), but not so useful for other businesses until they have something definite to put on it

- ▶ *Trade shows*: Good for small manufacturing and craft-based businesses. You will also need flyers and price lists

- ▶ *Advertising*: Helps if you are opening a shop or an eating establishment

- ▶ *Networking*: Excellent for any small business

For more advice on the advantages and disadvantages of these different marketing methods, and how to design them, see Chapter 4.

Write down your outline strategy, even if at this stage it is somewhat tentative.

▶ Start-up requirements

These will vary considerably, depending on the type of business you are setting up. Professional people may need office premises. Retailers and restaurants, pubs or cafés, for example, will need premises, as will manufacturing and craft-based businesses. You cannot really create rocking horses in the kitchen. People working from home (IT businesses, book-keepers, builders and decorators, plumbers and gardeners, for example) will not need premises, but all businesses will have some start-up requirements.

All businesses need stationery, some sort of IT, somewhere to store things, and probably an office desk and chair. For detailed advice on this, see Chapter 8.

Start from scratch, and write down everything you are going to need to get your business off the ground. A spider diagram might help. A home hairdresser, for example, could make a spider diagram starting like this:

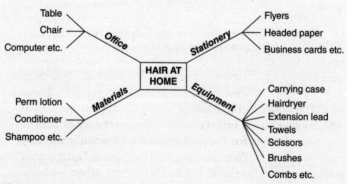

Figure 2.1 Start-up requirements

The spider's legs are the main 'headings' (stationery, equipment, materials, office) and its 'feet' are details which go with each leg – subheadings. You can mark all the things you already have, leaving you a list of those you must acquire.

Remember to include vehicles, including a reliable car, if you need one. And don't forget insurance if you are using your car for business purposes, and also insurance for premises, stock, materials and so on. Only you will know exactly what is essential. Write it all down, even if it does look daunting.

A business plan does help you to be realistic!

▶ People

Even if you are a sole trader, there may be people who 'help'. Your spouse, for example, may do the books and take bookings. Write a thumbnail sketch of everyone who is going to be involved in the business, in whatever their capacity, including yourself or yourselves.

Write down their background, experience, qualifications (if these are necessary to your business or enhance your credibility) and any other factors you think are important.

▶ Grey areas

You cannot predict everything that is likely to happen – practically every business has its peaks and troughs and 'grey' areas. Highlight those areas where you cannot be precise.

Retailers cannot possibly know exactly what their customer footfall will be, but they might know (and should know) seasonal trends. Summer sales and Christmas are usually good trading times. August is often a dead month for consultancies, as is December through to the New Year. If your business is gardening, there is little you can plant in January or February, but you can plan for the spring – although when it will arrive is unpredictable. Plan out your trading year as best you can, and plan for those times, predictable or not, when business is likely to be quiet.

It is useful, if you can, to have a plan B up your sleeve for those totally unpredictable events, such as a good customer going bust, or being taken over, a flu epidemic or a natural disaster. Are there additional resources you can call upon?

▶ The way forward

This is where you set a definite start date for your business – you will need to do so for your annual accounts anyway. Then you can begin to predict how long it will take to get your business firmly up and running. It could well take anything up to two years.

A **cash flow forecast** is a good tool for this, where you set your actual income and expenditure against your predicted income and expenditure. You can estimate what your expected income and expenditure is likely to be, but of course you cannot fill in the actual income and expenditure until you have been trading for a little while. Do the predictions as part of your business plan; at the very least it will help you to know how much your turnover must be for you to pay all the bills and survive – and eventually make a profit (Figure 2.2).

CASH FLOW FORECAST				
Month	January		February	
	BUDGET	ACTUAL	BUDGET	ACTUAL
Opening balance INCOMING – Sales – Other	–		–	
A Total receipts				
OUTGOING – Materials – Light/Heat – Rent/Rates – Wages/Salaries – Telephone/Postage etc.				
B Total payments				
A–B Balance (+ or –)				
CLOSING BALANCE (Transferred to next month)				

Figure 2.2 Cash flow forecast

Costing your service or product

COSTING YOUR SERVICE

How much should you charge? If you have been working in a larger business similar to your own, you may know roughly what those charges are, but you may not.

Consultants have the reputation of charging very large fees, and perhaps they do, but you are starting up your own small business and are unlikely to be able to charge as much, at least to begin with. Your start-up costs and overheads will probably not be very great; you are charging for your time and expertise. You might charge by the day or by the hour – these will be your **fees.** You can then add on **materials or services** which you have to buy in, and **expenses** such as travelling, hotels and subsistence. An office interior designer, for example, would need to cost out furnishings, lighting and so on, then add expenses and his or her time.

People offering home services, such as window cleaners, beauticians, therapists, home heating engineers, plumbers, builders, decorators and garden landscape practitioners, work in much the same way. There are fixed, often 'trade' purchases they pass on to their customers or clients, and then add the labour costs.

Try it now: Do a trial costing

If you are *providing* a service, do a trial costing, using Jay's Gardens below as an example. If you are *selling a product*, skip to Costing your product below.

Costing your service

Take a typical small job and cost it out. James, for example, is setting up a small gardening consultancy called Jay's Gardens. Presume he is working from home, and the job will take five days.

JAY'S GARDENS

Job

Laying a small patio with tubs

Overheads

A proportion of your business expenditure (on lighting, heating, stationery, etc.)

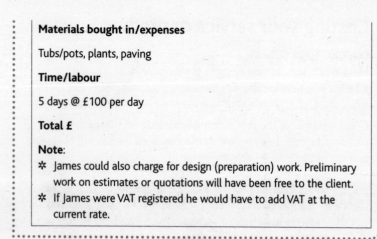

Materials bought in/expenses

Tubs/pots, plants, paving

Time/labour

5 days @ £100 per day

Total £

Note:

✳ James could also charge for design (preparation) work. Preliminary work on estimates or quotations will have been free to the client.

✳ If James were VAT registered he would have to add VAT at the current rate.

In both these cases the cost of your time is the most difficult to decide. Charge too much, and your work will dry up; charge too little and you are likely to be thought cheapskate and unprofessional. It depends on what the market will bear. Networking can be extremely useful here. You can find out from other people in the group roughly what they have had to pay for similar products or services.

COSTING YOUR PRODUCT

You are in business to make a profit. **Turnover** is the amount of money you take, month by month (your sales figures); **profit** is the amount of money you make after all expenditure is taken into account. So you need to charge the right amount to make enough to cover your costs, invest for the future and pay your own living expenses. It is often said that food retailers, starting the week on Monday, do not start to make a profit until Thursday.

MARK-UP AND MARGIN

The profit on any one item can be expressed in one of two ways:

1 as a percentage of the **cost price** (the price your supplier will charge), *or*

2 as a percentage of the **selling price** (the price at which you sell).

If based on the cost price it is called **mark-up**, if based on the selling price it is called **margin**.

This is how the calculations are done:

▶ **Mark-up**

$$\frac{(\text{Selling Price} - \text{Cost Price}) \times 100}{\text{Cost Price}}$$

On a calculator, key in the selling price minus the cost price. Divide the answer by the cost price and press the % key. Try it.

▶ **Margin**

$$\frac{(\text{Selling Price} - \text{Cost Price}) \times 100}{\text{Selling Price}}$$

On a calculator, key in the selling price minus the cost price. Divide the answer by the selling price and press the % key. Try it.

You will see that in percentage terms the mark-up is always greater than the margin. Why is it important to know this? Because, if you are negotiating with a supplier who quotes you a price on which it is said you could make a certain percentage profit, you need to know whether you are being quoted the mark-up or the margin percentage.

CALCULATING YOUR SELLING PRICE

Your selling price must take into account, for each item or each batch, a proportion of your overheads, which could include:

▶ salaries and wages

▶ National Insurance and other insurance

▶ light, heat, rent, rates, telephone, water, travelling, postage, insurance, etc.

▶ interest on loans and overdrafts

▶ materials

▶ machinery.

So, for any item or batch of items:

- ▶ Take the cost price (what you have paid your supplier).
- ▶ Add a proportion of your overheads.
- ▶ Add a mark-up percentage.
- ▶ Add VAT if applicable.

All this sounds rather complicated, so many people running a small shop or manufacturing business or eating establishment charge what they feel the market will bear. They base this on their experience and by comparing their charges with what their competitors charge. This could be an acceptable way of costing your product, which you can adjust as your business grows and you gain more experience.

Try it now: Calculate the selling price

Calculate the selling price of one single item you intend to sell, following this example:

OUR SHOP	
Cost price	£3.00
Add overheads at, say, 20% of cost price = £0.60	
	£3.60
Add a mark-up of, say, 50% of cost price = £1.50	
Selling price	£5.10
Add VAT if applicable	

Be aware that your business overheads may well be higher or lower than the percentage we have used. Likewise your mark-up percentage may be higher or lower. This is a very basic way of calculating your selling price, without taking into account discounts, early settlement terms and so on.

Arriving at the correct cost for your service or product is not easy, but you need to have some idea of what you will charge if you are to make a profit, particularly if you need to borrow money to get your business up and running.

All the figures in this section are ongoing, and will vary from item to item or job to job, over time. You may need to borrow quite a large sum as initial capital expenditure. The next section is about financing your business.

> **Remember this:** Cost your product or service materials correctly
>
> Costing your product or service materials correctly, remembering to include all applicable elements such as materials, labour charges and overheads, is a key factor in your small business success. In the end, it might come down to what the market will bear at the time.

Financing your business

Some businesses will need little start-up finance, particularly consultants and those working from home. Many businesses do need a loan or a grant to get going and, as always, there are many things to consider.

OBTAINING BUSINESS FINANCE

There are many sources of business finance, but which are the best to try?

▶ **Banks**

If you are in good standing, as they say, with your own bank, you might approach them first. They will often let you open a business account without any charge for the first year. However, some banks specialize in certain areas of business, so it might be wise to shop around. Your local business contacts and your accountant can help you here.

Building societies which have become banks can be helpful, particularly if you have a savings account with them. Those that are still 'mutual' tend to be less geared up to deal with small businesses.

▶ **Venture capital**

What about venture capital, and what is it? Venture capital is what people invest in your business, and in return they will take a stake in your business. It may be as simple as members of the family becoming shareholders if you are a limited company – they may expect to be paid interest, will almost certainly expect you to repay the loan at some point and will probably expect to be paid dividends out of your profits. Be careful in choosing family or friends: you and they can fall out over business decisions, sometimes with long-term consequences.

However, venture capital is generally considered to be provided by other well-heeled businesspeople who are prepared to back your business venture. Be very hesitant before you go down that route, unless you are an inventor, perhaps – a venture capitalist is a last resort.

▶ Grants

Your new business might qualify for local or EU grants, particularly if you are in a development area. Approach your local council, your county council, or the Federation of Small Businesses for advice. Your local Chamber of Commerce might help you, too. You can also try the Department for Business, Enterprise and Regulatory Reform, formerly the Department of Trade and Industry (DTI), which is of great help to businesses, both large and small, on many business aspects.

▶ Remortgaging your house

Some people consider doing this to finance their business, but very few do it and succeed. The best advice is 'Don't do it'. There has to be another way. Consider getting off the ground in a more modest way, perhaps concentrating on one aspect of your proposed business to start with and expanding gradually into other areas as circumstances permit.

▶ Crowd funding or peer funding

Crowd funding or peer funding is a relatively new way of funding a range of businesses, including very small ones. Various websites put those who wish to lend money in touch with those who need to borrow. Search for crowd funding on the Web, which will lead you to a variety of websites. It is well worth considering, particularly for start-ups.

PRESENTING YOUR CASE

You have chosen your lender and have made an appointment to see someone in your local branch, often called something like a 'Small Business Manager' or 'Small Business Advisor'. These days it is unlikely to be your bank manager. There are certain things which this person will want you to tell them: what your proposed business is about; how much you want to borrow; what collateral you can offer, and how you propose to repay the loan.

▶ What your proposed business is about

This is where your business plan comes in. If possible, use the starter pack supplied by the lender you are now approaching. Make sure it is well presented and take enough copies for everyone at the meeting. You may like to take your accountant with you, who could add a certain amount of weight and credibility to your proposal. You could also take photographs or designs, if those are applicable – anything to persuade your lender that this is a serious proposition with a sound basis. Take your business cards and any relevant marketing material.

▶ How much you want to borrow

You will already have outlined your initial capital costs in your business plan, but there are other items to add in. On a separate sheet list the initial capital costs, the start-up expenses and the ongoing costs, with an estimate of the total for each section and the full amount you want to borrow. Include the following:

▶ **Initial capital costs** Initial capital costs are often one-off payments to get the business off the ground. If you are setting up a small industrial unit, a craft-based workshop, a restaurant, tea room or coffee shop, or any kind of retail outlet, you might need to think about:

  ▷ décor and decoration

  ▷ lighting, heating and ventilation

  ▷ equipment and tools

  ▷ fire precautions and security installations

  ▷ telecommunications

▷ office furniture and equipment

▷ fixtures and fittings

▷ furniture for clients or customers

▷ vehicles

▷ stock.

All this can easily come to between £20,000 and £30,000.

▶ **Start-up expenses** Other, less tangible, items could include:

▷ stationery design and supply

▷ marketing

▷ website design and maintenance

▷ a domain name

▷ subscriptions to professional or trade bodies and business clubs

▷ wrapping materials

▷ packaging materials.

▶ **Ongoing costs** These will gradually be covered by your profits, but you need to cover yourself for, say, the first three months before the business starts to make any serious money. These costs include:

▷ rent and rates

▷ staff costs

▷ National Insurance

▷ telephone

▷ electricity

▷ water

▷ insurance

▷ interest on your loan.

Another £10,000 or £20,000 could easily bring your initial financial requirements to £40,000 or £50,000. You may have some money you can put into the business yourself, perhaps a legacy or some redundancy money. Deduct this from the total start-up figure and you will arrive at the amount you need to borrow.

▶ What collateral you can offer

Collateral is a way of guaranteeing the repayment of the loan you are asking for – someone, or something, which backs up your loan. You could use your house, but not without great thought and discussion with your accountant. This is not remortgaging your house, but allowing the lender to have a charge on it. This means that if your business fails and your only asset is your home, your lender could require you to sell the house to repay the loan. Imagine what effect this would have on you and your family.

You might be able to get a member of your family to guarantee the loan. If you are young, your parents might be a good bet! Put yourself in your lender's shoes and ask yourself, 'If this borrower's business fails, how will I get my money back?' Be prepared to answer this question.

HOW YOU REPAY THE LOAN

You will usually not be expected to repay the loan in one lump sum. The capital you have borrowed could be paid off in stage payments, a chunk at a time. You will usually pay the interest monthly, and you should have allowed for this in the first three months in your calculations. This is where you will need a cash flow forecast.

A **cash flow forecast** is an educated estimate of the income and expenditure of your business over a given period. Alongside are the actual income and expenditure figures for that same period. Obviously you cannot complete the second half until you have been trading for a little while. Your cash flow forecast could look like the one in Chapter 7.

Even if you do not need to borrow money, a cash flow forecast is a very useful business tool, which you can do manually or electronically.

If you have doubts about being able to make a repayment, talk to your accountant without delay and arrange for the two of you to meet the lender. Work out beforehand suggested solutions to the problem for your lender to consider and respond to. The lender will usually listen sympathetically to what you propose, if you approach them early enough. After all, they want to get their money back!

Try it now: Financing your business

This exercise is relevant if you need to borrow money to get your business started. Use the headings below to help you to prepare for a meeting with a lender.

YOUR BUSINESS NAME

Name of lender: (bank)

Address of lender:

Contact details:
* Business manager
* Telephone number
* Email

Amount you want to borrow:

What to take with you – enough copies of:
* Business plan
* Photographs, designs, etc.
* Loan calculation
* Business cards
* Marketing material
* Cash flow forecast

The lowest amount you can accept:

(You may need to negotiate.)

Name of your accountant:

This is serious business planning – do it well!

Premises

WORKING FROM HOME

For some people, working from home is out of the question, because of manufacturing processes or the storage space required, for instance, but for many it can be a good starting point. The types of business which are suitable for working from home are likely to be:

▶ consultancy

▶ teaching/training

▶ 'cottage' industry (e.g. crafts, food)

▶ professions (e.g. accountants, therapists, architects).

Sometimes a good business address is essential to your image; in this case an obviously residential address would be a handicap.

▶ Customer and client access

If yours is the type of business where you go to your clients or customers – goods made at home and delivered or services rendered on other people's premises perhaps – a home base could work quite well.

It is essential that your customers are able to get in touch with you quickly and easily by phone or email at times convenient to them. You also have to guard your own privacy, however, and make it clear that business is done in business hours, whatever those may be. For example, if your business hours exclude mornings, and you work afternoons, evenings and weekends, this must be made clear to your customers. Home hairdressing could be an example here.

If your business requires your customers to come to you, if only occasionally (consultants or accountants, for instance), it is very important to be able to receive them in a business-like atmosphere, with all the privacy they would expect from business premises. Parking should be convenient, if possible, and the entry to your home easy and pleasant. Being greeted by a doorbell which does not work, a barking dog and a noisy child is not a good introduction to a business atmosphere.

If you are doing business with customers in your home, a separate office or study is highly desirable.

▶ Space

If your business is a cottage industry, you obviously need enough space in which to process what you are making. A shed or garage can sometimes be used. Remember that you will also need storage space for:

▶ **equipment**: materials, including wrapping or packing materials

▶ **tools**: the tools of your trade

▶ **deliveries**: items ready for delivery to customers

You will need good access for getting these things in and out of your home without causing annoyance to the rest of your household or your neighbours.

You will also need space for the office side of the business. Equipment such as photocopiers and desktops takes up quite a bit of room. A separate office is ideal, if possible. Remember that you will need a phone in the 'office' as well as where you are working, but your mobile is available anywhere.

If you are supplying a service, as opposed to a product, from your home, less space is needed, but you still need to be able to store paper, files, office machinery and so on. Take account of this, and try to keep your business space and your private space separate.

▶ Overheads

You need to be clear, as soon as possible, what proportion of the overheads on your home you can claim for business purposes. You should be able to claim a proportion of your:

- ▶ lighting and heating
- ▶ telephone
- ▶ security
- ▶ cleaning

} if necessary

Reckon on being able to claim anything to do with the business, not with the house. If you start claiming for rates or water rates, you may be liable to capital gains tax when you sell the house. The council tax should not be affected at all by the fact that you work from home.

Check with your accountant what proportion of household expenses can be deemed to be for business use and how this should be recorded in the books. For example, you should be able to claim VAT (if you are VAT-registered) on your business phone calls, and on a proportion of any telephone rental charges.

If you have cleaning help in the home, some of this payment might be offset as a business expense, but take care that your cleaning person does not become an employee for personal tax or National Insurance (NI) purposes.

Other things you might be able to claim for are a guard dog, installing security devices, extra telephone points and secretarial services by other members of the household, but check with your accountant first.

You need to be sure, when setting up your business at home, that you are not altering the use of the property or part of it from residential to light industrial. Check with the local authority bye-laws and a solicitor who is fully conversant with these.

WORKSHOPS, WAREHOUSES AND FACTORIES

If you are dealing with products, as opposed to services, you will often need to rent premises in which to work. Premises available can range from small workshops of no more than 50 square metres (500 sq. ft) to small factories, depending on requirements. It is unusual for someone starting out in business to need a large factory straight away, but it is possible.

A warehouse is normally used for storage purposes only – storage of materials before processing, storage of deliveries ready for despatch or storage if you are the middle person between the seller and the buyer.

▶ Size

The size depends on what you are producing, the size of the machinery or equipment you use and the amount of space needed for immediate storage of materials, packaging, wrapping and the finished product ready for despatch. It is sometimes more cost-effective to rent a slightly larger workshop which will accommodate all these requirements comfortably than to rent a separate storage area or warehouse.

When calculating the size required, remember to allow adequate space for the people who are going to work there, for facilities for those people (personal belongings storage, refreshments and so on) and for a certain amount of office space. Even if you are doing the books elsewhere (at home, for example), you will need a space on site for processing paperwork; this space will need to house a desktop or space for your laptop. You will certainly need somewhere to put the phone.

▶ Access

You need easy access to your premises for:

▶ yourself

▶ your staff

▶ deliveries

▶ despatch.

Make sure you can get into your premises when you want to – round the clock if necessary. Make sure that your staff can get in if you are not there for any reason.

Consider access for large delivery vehicles, particularly if you buy in bulk. What unloading facilities are there?

Is there adequate parking for you, your staff and your own vehicle(s) for despatching goods? What are the loading facilities for your own vehicles? Are lifts available if necessary?

Try making a list of all the people and products which will be going in and out of the premises and check for each whether they can get in and out in a cost-effective and practical way.

▶ Security

What security measures are in force to protect the premises you are going to rent? If you have 24-hour access, who else does? How secure are the windows and doors? How secure will your merchandise or products be while being unloaded and loaded? What lighting arrangements are there? What security system will you be allowed to install, if you need to? What security arrangements can be made for personal belongings?

Check the security:

- ▶ outside the premises
- ▶ inside the premises
- ▶ when receiving deliveries
- ▶ when despatching deliveries
- ▶ of personal property and vehicles
- ▶ of company vehicles.

▶ Health and safety

Make sure you are aware of the provisions of the Health and Safety at Work etc. Act 1974 (HASAWA) and its subsequent workplace regulations. Check:

- ▶ COSHH Regulations 1989 (Control of Substances Hazardous to Health)
- ▶ machine guards and rules and regulations for cleaning and maintenance

- fire exits
- fire appliances
- evacuation procedures
- protective clothing, if necessary.

If you are an employer, you are responsible for providing safe and healthy working conditions for your staff. The Health and Safety Executive (HSE) publishes many leaflets and books, several of which are free. (Telephone 0845 3450055 or go to www.hse.gov.uk)

If your workshop, factory or warehouse is part of an industrial complex, you need to check the health and safety regulations relating to that complex, and that you are able to comply with them.

Remember to check the safety of your company vehicles and to have them regularly serviced, particularly if they are driven by someone other than yourself.

Costs

It is impossible to suggest a fair rent for premises because this varies so widely in different parts of the country, and often in different parts of the same town.

It is helpful to make a list of what is essential to you when searching for premises and what is desirable. Also, considering your cash flow forecast, set a maximum rent you are prepared to pay, and stick to it. Remember that you might have to pay a one-off premium, sometimes returnable at the termination of the tenancy, as well as rent in advance when you agree to rent the premises.

Check whether the rent quoted is inclusive or exclusive of such items as rates, communal services (security guard, window cleaner, for instance), building maintenance and so on. Are there any hidden extras?

It is not always the cheapest rent which is the most economical. Balance your needs against your preferences; if the property does not meet the essentials you require, go elsewhere: be prepared to pay a bit more if necessary, but not beyond the maximum you have set yourself.

OFFICE PREMISES

If you are offering a service, it might not be appropriate to work from home because of lack of space. Perhaps you are in partnership, and it would not be sensible to work from the home of either or any of the partners. In these cases you will be looking for office accommodation to rent.

Much of what has been said about workshops, warehouses and factories applies here. You need to consider:

▶ what size premises you need

▶ access to your office

▶ security

▶ health and safety

▶ cost.

There are, however, additional matters to be considered when renting office accommodation.

▶ Image

A good address and prestigious offices are vital to some businesses. For example, an interior design consultancy needs an address and office premises and furniture in keeping with its up-market image. It is worth looking for an office in areas which are being gentrified as well as those which are well established as prestige areas. If you can get into an area which is about to move up-market early, so much the better.

Again it will depend on whether clients come to you or you go to them, but it is unusual for your offices never to be visited by potential clients, whatever your business. Therefore you need offices into which you will not be ashamed to welcome visitors, without going to unnecessary expense. This is tied up with the next section on services.

▶ Services

Sometimes office accommodation comes with extra services, such as cleaning, window cleaning, reception, switchboard, fax, and mail in and out. You should check which of these services is included in the rent, if any.

When visiting the premises, if it is an office block of which you intend to rent one small part, note how well the reception area is maintained, whether the grass (if any) is cut, whether the plants are tended and how well you are received by the receptionist. These are all indicative of how well the building is run and this is an indication of the image that will be conveyed to your own clients.

If you are planning to rent premises above shops, visit during the busiest time of the day so that you can judge the noise levels or smells from neighbouring premises to see whether they are acceptable.

▶ Accommodation

When calculating the square footage of accommodation you require, remember to take account of the provisions of the Offices, Shops and Railway Premises Act 1963, which lays down, among other things, how much working space each person should have, and what toilet facilities should be available.

Look for adequate power points for your office machinery and desk lamps, and check that the temperature can be regulated so that it is not too cold for the people or too hot for the equipment.

Office workers normally require either good car parking facilities or easy access to shops and public transport.

FINDING OUT WHAT IS AVAILABLE

The main sources of information about what is available in the way of business premises to rent are:

- ▶ your local library

- ▶ estate agents who specialize in that type of property

- ▶ local authorities, for premises owned and rented by them
- ▶ local business organizations
- ▶ your own observations.

▶ Libraries

If your local library is a good one – that is, it offers an up-to-date reference section and knowledgeable staff – you have a highly prized source of information. It can supply you with copies of:

- ▶ specialist books on finding premises
- ▶ lists of professional advisers
- ▶ lists of premises available
- ▶ publications on how to choose and rent premises
- ▶ the Land Registers which show publicly owned land which is under-utilized
- ▶ the *Business Location Handbook* by area in the UK
- ▶ enterprise or development zones, planning offices, etc.

▶ Estate agents

The library will probably have a list of estate agents which specialize in business premises. Local business directories are helpful.

An agent with local knowledge is an advantage. Test by asking about a property of which you have personal knowledge to see what the agent has to say about it.

▶ Local authorities

Local authorities often own large areas of property and are prepared to rent office and manufacturing accommodation to small businesses. They also hold records of planning applications, so you can look up where developments are likely to occur and therefore where premises are likely to be available. They will also have details of business parks and industrial estates. The local telephone directory will normally give some indication of the correct department to approach.

▶ **Your own observation**

Keep a lookout yourself for likely empty premises. Look above shops and in basements, particularly for office accommodation. Nearby shops and offices will often know who the landlord is.

Watch for signs of private and public developments – premises gutted or new access roads being built. A property which is being run down might be a good short-term bet for you, because terms are likely to be favourable. See Chapter 10 for information about retail premises.

? Self-assessment: Your premises

Be clear about the premises you need to start up your business. Work through this tick box questionnaire.

	YES	NO
1 Are you working from home?	☐	☐
If YES, answer questions 2–4.		
If NO, go to question 5.		
2 Have you a separate office or study?	☐	☐
3 Is there enough space for:		
✱ equipment?	☐	☐
✱ materials (if applicable)?	☐	☐
✱ tools (if applicable)?	☐	☐
✱ items ready for delivery (if applicable)?	☐	☐
✱ stationery?	☐	☐
✱ files?	☐	☐
4 Do you know what proportion of the overheads on your home you can claim for business purposes?	☐	☐

5 Does your business need a workshop, warehouse or factory? ☐ ☐

If YES, answer questions 6–11.

If NO, go to question 12.

6 Do you know the size of premises you need? ☐ ☐

7 Is there easy access for:

✳ yourself? ☐ ☐

✳ your staff? ☐ ☐

✳ deliveries? ☐ ☐

✳ despatch? ☐ ☐

8 Do you need 24-hour access? ☐ ☐

9 Is there good security:

✳ outside the premises? ☐ ☐

✳ inside the premises? ☐ ☐

✳ when receiving deliveries? ☐ ☐

✳ when despatching deliveries? ☐ ☐

✳ of personal property and vehicles? ☐ ☐

✳ of company vehicles? ☐ ☐

10 Do the premises conform to the Health and Safety at Work etc. Act 1974 (HASAWA)? ☐ ☐

11 Have you made a list of what is essential and what is desirable? ☐ ☐

12 Does your business need office premises only? ☐ ☐

If YES, go to questions 13–17.

If NO, ignore the rest of this questionnaire.

13 Do you need a prestigious office address? ☐ ☐

14 Are all the services you need included in the rent? ☐ ☐

15	Do the premises conform to the Offices, Shops and Railway Premises Act 1963?	☐	☐
16	Is there easy access and parking for you and your staff?	☐	☐
17	Is there good security?	☐	☐

Focus points

By the time you reach the end of this chapter you should have:

* decided on your method of trading
* made a business plan
* decided what to charge for your product or service
* secured your start-up finance if necessary
* taken the first steps to organizing your business premises.

Next step

An essential part of your initial planning is making decisions about your image. Chapter 3 guides you through consideration of your business name, your letterhead and email design, your publicity material and the image portrayed by your premises, your vehicles and your personnel, even if it is only you. See yourself as others see you.

Your image

In this chapter you will learn:

▶ *How to develop a company image that suits your business and expresses its reliability, competence and success*

▶ *How to choose a name and design a logo*

▶ *How to write effective and professional letters and emails*

▶ *How to develop a smart, professional image through your premises, vehicles and staff, as well as through your own manner, appearance, etc.*

We hear a lot about image in political parties, with discussions on whether a party's or a person's image is attractive to voters, although their policies lack substance. The same can be said about a business, its product or service (its substance), and its image. Image does attract people. Think how much time women, and men, take making themselves look good, but how, if the underlying person is flawed, any relationship is unlikely to last. This is how conmen (and women) trade – on their image.

So, unless your own business is soundly based, offering products or services which customers or clients want, with good value for money, your business will not last. This does not mean that image is unimportant – it is. A good, appropriate image first attracts people and then, provided the image is maintained, helps to keep them.

What is your own vision of your business? High-class and exclusive, or cheap and cheerful? It's probably somewhere between the two.

Self-assessment: The image of your business

This seems a simple exercise, but is more difficult than you might think. Write down a list of adjectives (adjectives describe nouns) which best describe your image of your business. Here are some examples to get you going:

Reliable	Careful	Proactive
Fashionable	Imaginative	Cutting edge
Fast-moving	Colourful	Caring
Professional	Participative	Meticulous
Arty	Inspirational	Exclusive

An accountant, for example, would wish to be seen as 'meticulous', but not necessarily 'colourful'. How far does 'reliable' (a rather pedestrian image) contradict 'cutting edge' (which gives a feeling of an up-to-the-minute, perhaps risky enterprise)?

When you, yourself, have a good idea of the image you want to convey, you can start applying it to the various facets of your business which, in their turn, convey it to your customers and clients.

Your name and logo

YOUR NAME

What are you going to call your business? Sometimes the right name will come to you very quickly, but some businesses have to agonize over it and, eventually, change it. Remember Royal Mail changing its name to Consignia? It never really caught on, because it did not mean anything to most people, and was difficult to remember. And that's one of the keys to a good name – it must mean something easily understood and be easy to remember and pronounce.

Many of the household names, such as Boots, Ford, W. H. Smith, Marks & Spencer and Moss Bros do not immediately say what these companies are about – they do not *mean* anything. But they are so well established that everyone knows what they sell. Marks & Spencer became known as Marks & Sparks, but now it is M&S, which is a fashionable way of naming a company – by initials. So British Telecom becomes BT, International Business Machines is IBM, the British Broadcasting Corporation is BBC, His Master's Voice is HMV and so on.

Yours is a new business, so calling it by initials might not be such a good idea. What would CHP mean to anyone? It stands for Chester House Productions, which, to anyone in that line of business, would convey that it is a film, theatre or television production company.

Puns or quirky names such as The Right Plaice, for a fish and chip shop, or Baguetti Junction (yes, it does exist!) are fine for certain establishments, but would that type of name suit your particular business? Look again at the assessment and decide what type of name is best for you.

What do you think of the names of the two companies used as examples in Chapters 1 and 2? Jay's Gardens and Affordable Fashion? Do they immediately convey what those businesses are about? If James had called his business Jay's Nursery you would not know whether he was talking about plants or babies, and, anyway, a plant nursery is quite different from a gardening consultancy.

Many consultancies call themselves by the sole proprietor's name and add 'and Associates', such as Michael Robinson and

Associates, or just Michael Robinson Associates. This conveys to people seeking their services that they are a consultancy in association with others. They do not necessarily employ people, but call upon associates when they need them.

You often see names like Peter Crockford & Son, or Sons, or Stanton Bros (for Brothers). This conveys that it is a family firm, often of long standing, and is used by butchers, builders, and painters and decorators. You rarely see Caroline Mitchell and Daughters anywhere.

Bear in mind that, as well as meaning something, your business name must be easy to pronounce in the UK and in other countries if you intend to trade Europe-wide or worldwide. A name like Thwaites Medical Supplies is very difficult for the French, for example. Patel Provisions, on the other hand, is easy to say in many languages, even though it comes from the Indian subcontinent, and tells you it is probably a convenience store or corner shop. Also it is easy to spell for website purposes.

Bear in mind, too, that there are certain legal constraints. If yours is a limited company it must have Limited or Ltd or PLC somewhere in the name or on the stationery. Some regional names have obtained protection for their products, such as champagne and Melton Mowbray pork pies, and you may not use them. Names similar to well-known names can be liable to prosecution for infringement of copyright. Call your small company, which sells beauty products, Charnell Number Five, because your address happens to be 5 High Street, and you could imagine that the House of Chanel would immediately seek legal advice! It's worth checking with the Patent Office or the Federation of Small Businesses before you register your business with its new name.

One last thing before you fully decide on your business name. Words with hard consonants in them, such as the 'k', 'd', 't' or 'q' sound, have a certain bite, or sharpness, to them, which makes them sound immediate and fast-moving. Kall Kwik is a good example of this. The soft consonants like 's', 'f' and 'p' convey a gentler, more leisurely image. Sanderson, for example, gives a feeling of soft fabric and wallpaper.

What is your business name going to be?

Your logo

Not every business has a logo as such – that is, a graphic of some sort. Many rely on just their name or initials. As you walk round your local shopping area, look consciously at logos. Are they instantly recognizable? Do they enhance the business image? Some companies' logos change over the years, while still keeping the fundamental message. The AA, for example, now has lettering which is much more modern-looking than its original, but it still says AA and is in yellow and black. Ford's logo is just as it has always been, in what some might think is old-fashioned lettering, but it's universally recognized, so why change it?

WHAT OTHER PEOPLE DO

Collect letterheads, business cards, junk mail, adverts and any other business paperwork, particularly those in the same line of business as yourself, including those of your competitors. Do the same for emails and websites, and adverts on the Internet. Look at them quickly, do not study them for too long, and decide what sort of image that business conveys to you. It gives you a starting point.

COLOUR

What sort of colour is right for your business? Should it be vibrant and exciting or more restrained and tasteful? Red is very powerful and in-your-face. Combined with yellow, it is startling. Red with green is no good for colour-blind people. Red on blue is difficult to read. Green is the colour of nature, eco-friendly and fresh. As with all colours, it comes in many different shades. Some people think green an unlucky colour, particularly at a wedding. Blue is thought of as a communicator's colour, while yellow is full of sunshine, light and cheerful. Yellow does not always stand out very well, unless it is combined with black. The easiest to read is considered to be black on yellow.

What about the background colour of your stationery and flyers? White is the most common background colour and is fine for most businesses. Printed emails always come out in white anyway, unless your recipient asks their system to print in colour. A brightly coloured flyer can be very eye-catching from a distance, but can you read what is written on it? Does that shocking-pink A4 poster convey the true nature of your business? Perhaps it does!

Case study: Letterheads

Look at these letterheads for our example small businesses, Jay's Gardens and Affordable Fashion.

Jay's Gardens
Design, landscaping, planting

Little Oaks, Church Lane, Stratton, WN14 6FP

Telephone: 01765 321432

Email: JamesG@tiscali.com

Website: www.jaysgardens.co.uk

Figure 3.1

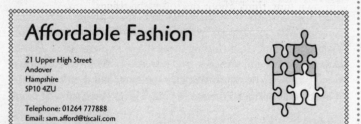

Affordable Fashion

21 Upper High Street
Andover
Hampshire
SP10 4ZU

Telephone: 01264 777888
Email: sam.afford@tiscali.com

Figure 3.2 Letterhead design

Jay's Gardens is lettering only, but it is green (although we cannot show that here) and in an unusual font called ITC Highlander std. Does it convey a 'gardening' image? By contrast, Affordable Fashion, although we can only represent it here in black and white, actually has a more colourful logo that looks like jigsaw pieces, conveying that it is up to date and the idea that you can put all sorts of things together to make a colourful whole.

These logos were not designed by professional graphic artists, but perhaps you need the services of someone to advise you. Your local printer is a good source of help and advice, but you may think your logo design is important enough to seek the services of a professional designer, which can be expensive. Whether you design your own or get help from others, these are some things to do or think about.

Generally, the lighter colours such as cream, white or possibly light grey are suitable background colours for business stationery, but remember that your name and logo should be used throughout the range: on letterheads; business cards; invoices; flyers; posters; website; envelopes even. Will all these identify themselves as coming from your business?

TYPEFACE (OR FONT)

There are, literally, thousands of fonts; some are very arty, others more solid and dependable-looking; some have flourishes, others are plain. Look at the examples you have collected and pick out those which best convey the company's image, as you see it, and are readable. Then have a glance down all the fonts available on your software; there are those which stand out and those which almost disappear. When choosing your own font, think about the following things.

▶ **Serif or sans serif?**

Look at any printed material and you will see that in some cases each letter has little extra 'bits' on it, or not. These little extra bits are called serifs.

▶ Times New Roman is a typical serif font.

▶ Arial is a typical sans serif (without serifs) font.

Which is better? Research has shown that for the majority of readers a serif typeface is easier to read than a sans serif because it flows along the line. On the other hand, readers such as engineers, technical people and medical people are used to a sans serif font. Also, sans serif looks more clean, clinical and up to date.

▶ **The x height**

Look at the words below and you will see there are two lines within which the majority of letters are confined:

<u>spring</u>   <u>box</u>

The line at the top is called the x height, where the letter 'x' finishes. The letters 'p' and 'g' go below the bottom line, and these extensions are called descenders. The letter 'b' has an ascender.

▶ Ascenders and descenders

Some fonts have a very high x height, which can make the font difficult to read. So choose a font which has normal ascenders and descenders, unless you want your typeface to emphasize the vertical.

▶ Capital letters and lowercase

When you read, you recognize the shape of the word. Take

spring   and   string

for example. Written in lower case they have only one letter difference, but are different shapes. If written in upper case (capital letters), the shape is the same: they are both boxes.

SPRING

and

STRING

The worst thing you can do is have a whole sentence in upper case, underlined, which only emphasizes the box shape. Bold is better. Your business name will not be a sentence, but it needs to be legible, so think about upper- and lower-case letters. Have a look at motorway signs. They are in lower case, sans serif, with normal ascenders and descenders – easily readable from a distance. (Incidentally, capital and small letters are called upper and lower case because, in the original typewriters in the 19th century, the typewriter arms bearing the letters were, literally, in two cases, one upper and one lower.)

PRINTERS

Having chosen your logo, including the font, make sure it will print out both on your own printer and on the machines used by a professional printer. Sometimes your professional printer will not have your particular font and will need to import it from your computer, provided they have a licence to do so.

Letter and email design and layout

You have chosen your name and designed your logo, so now you have to think about the design and layout of your letterhead and your emails. Remember that whatever you design here will have to be replicated on invoices, statements, estimates, quotations and business cards, to make sure your image is carried through. When someone picks up one of your documents, you want them to know immediately that it is from you. That is one of the problems with emails: they all look the same when they are printed out at the other end; but you can do something about it, as you will see later in this chapter.

LETTERHEAD DESIGN

You may not write many letters as such – emails are the most likely form of correspondence – but you will need letter paper from time to time. What should it include, and how should it be laid out?

There are certain things your headed paper *must* include:

▶ 'Limited', 'Ltd' or 'PLC' or 'Plc' somewhere if yours is a limited company or a public limited company (unlikely at this stage)

▶ your company registration number, if your company is registered at companies house

▶ your VAT registration number if you are VAT-registered

- the names of all partners
- the names of all or one of the directors.

There are things your headed paper *should* include:

- your registered address and your contact address if these are different
- your telephone number(s)
- your fax number, if applicable
- your email address
- your website address, if you wish
- your Facebook and/or Twitter logo.

Where should all this information go? You can choose from several arrangements, which tend to go in fashions:

- name and logo across the top of the paper, centred
- contact details centred immediately below
- name and logo left-aligned (against the left-hand margin)
- contact details underneath
- name and logo right-aligned (against the right-hand margin)
- contact details underneath
- name and logo across the top of the paper
- contact details at the bottom (has become quite fashionable)
- name of partners or directors at the bottom
- company registration number and VAT registration number right at the bottom

Have a look at Quantock Fashions Plc's letterhead, one of Affordable Fashion's suppliers. It is quite simple and leaves plenty of space for whatever needs to be written on it; it can be used for letters, invoices, statements and quotations, as necessary. Also, have a look at the other business documents you have collected and see what appeals to you and what matches your image.

Quantock Fashions Plc

Taunton Road
Bridgwater
Somerset
TA7 5DQ

Telephone: 01278 687422
Email: quantockfashions@aol.com
www.quantockfashions.co.uk

VAT Registration No: 654 3219 87
Directors: David Cook, Sophie Grainger, Timothy Saunders

Figure 3.3 Example letterhead

Try it now: Design your letterhead

Even if you are going to seek professional advice, it is wise to go with some idea of what you want. Many people design their own.

Decide:
* Where your name (and logo) will be
* Where your contact details will be
* Where any partners' or directors' names will be
* Where any registration number will be

It looks old-fashioned to use punctuation marks, except an apostrophe or a hyphen where they are appropriate in, for example, 6 Queen's Square or Ashton-under-Lyne. (Note: no space before or after the hyphen.) Hyphens join but dashes (the same symbol on the keyboard) separate. A dash has one space before and one space after it; a hyphen has none.

You have chosen the font for your business name. Will you use the same for your contact and other details? If your name is in a fancy serif font, it might look good to have the other details in a simpler, but compatible, sans serif font. Try several out and look at the result.

Finally, print your letterhead out in colour on your chosen paper, and look critically at the end result. What does it say about your image?

Remember this: Let it breathe

Leave enough space for the content of the letter – don't crowd it.

LETTER LAYOUT

Once you are satisfied with your letterhead, decide on what the content of a letter should look like, because this will also add to or detract from your image. Letters are usually fairly formal documents, unlike emails, so need to look professional without being old-fashioned.

Look at Figure 3.4, which shows a formal letter from Quantock Fashions Plc to Sam informing her that their business is moving to a bigger site in Taunton to accommodate their expansion. On the following page are notes on each part of the letter; these are conventions, not rules.

Quantock Fashions Plc

Taunton Road
Bridgwater
Somerset
TA7 5DQ

Telephone: 01278 687422
Email: quantockfashions@aol.com
www.quantockfashions.co.uk

Customer No: 3654AF

3 October 2015

Ms Samantha Holdness
Affordable Fashion
21 Upper High Street
Andover
Hampshire
SP10 4ZU

Dear Ms Holdness

Change of address

We are pleased to inform you that, due to expansion, we are moving to larger premises on the other side of Bridgwater.

As from 1 November 2015 our address will be:

Quantock Fashions Plc
Quantock Industrial Estate
Glastonbury Road
Bridgwater
Somerset
TA8 5WJ

Our other details, telephone, email and website, remain the same. Our move has been carefully planned, so that your deliveries should not be affected in any way.

We look forward to receiving your next order.

Yours sincerely

Daniel Kershaw
Sales Manager

VAT Registration No: 654 3219 87
Directors: David Cook, Sophie Grainger, Timothy Saunders

Figure 3.4 Example formal letter

- ▶ **References.** Put your reference and the recipient's reference number, if applicable.

- ▶ **The date.** Write as 5 February 2015. This way there can be no mistake about the date. 02.10 would mean 2 October in the UK, whereas in the USA it would mean 10 February. Make sure the computer writes it as you want it. No 'rd', 'nd' or 'th', which looks old-fashioned.

- ▶ **The recipient's name.** Be sure to get this absolutely correct. Titles (Mr, Mrs, Miss, Ms, Dr, etc.) can be confusing, so either ring up and check what the correct title is, especially for a woman, or do not use a title at all: just write Samantha Holdness. This form of address is becoming much more usual.

- ▶ **The recipient's job title and address.** These must also be totally correct. No punctuation at all so far.

- ▶ **The salutation ('Dear…').** If you do not know the person, use their full name 'Dear Ms Holdness'; if you know them, you can write 'Dear Samantha' or 'Dear Sam'. If you have not used a title, you can write 'Dear Samantha Holdness'. It is still usual to use 'Dear…' rather than 'Hi!' in a letter. If you do not know the person's name, use a job title, such as 'Dear Sales Manager'. 'Dear Sir or Madam' is a last resort.

- ▶ **A heading, in bold, left-aligned, lower case.** This immediately tells the recipient what the letter is about. If the letter is about several subjects, use more headings further down the page. Always leave more space above a heading than below it, so that the heading belongs to the text. The word 'Re:' is unnecessary.

- ▶ **The body of the letter** is better left-aligned and ragged right (not fully justified).

- ▶ **The first paragraph** should refer to something that has been the trigger to write the letter. 'Thank you for your letter of…' is OK, but rather uninteresting. Try 'I was pleased/ disappointed/puzzled to see from your letter of…'.

- ▶ **The next paragraph(s)** should set out the main points of what you want to say. Indent for emphasis.

- ▶ **The last paragraph** should be clear about the next step(s), if any.

- ▶ **A courteous ending** is fine, but write something different from 'Please do not hesitate to contact me', which is so often used it has become boring. Instead, try something like 'I look forward to meeting you on...' or 'I shall be in the office next week if you want to contact me.'

- ▶ **The complimentary close.** Convention says that 'Dear Sir or Madam' should be followed by 'Yours faithfully' and 'Dear (name)' should be followed by 'Yours sincerely'. You will avoid the former if at all possible, so will rarely use 'Yours faithfully'. 'Regards' or 'Kind regards' is becoming much more usual. 'Yours truly' is used more in the USA.

- ▶ **Sign** your letter personally, in ink, if your image requires it. Use blue or black, not green (which accountants tend to use) or red, which is thought of as aggressive. If you are a 'purple' type of person, well, you are that type of person and that is what your image will convey.

- ▶ **Add your job title** as appropriate, and if you are a woman add Mrs, Miss or Ms in brackets, out of courtesy to your reader – that is, if you want a title used at all.

- ▶ If you are **enclosing anything** write 'Enc.' or 'Encs' at the bottom and list the enclosures. It is helpful your end when stuffing the envelope and helpful the other end when opening it.

- ▶ Finally, if you are **sending copies** to anyone, write 'Copy to...'; 'c.c.' stands for carbon copy.

So much for a formal letter. No wonder people use emails!

EMAIL DESIGN AND LAYOUT

Many emails are informal messages between business people who know each other well. Some, however, need to be more formal.

▶ Name and address

Email design is standardized. You know exactly the email address of your recipient and must, of course, get it exactly right or the email will bounce back. The same applies to copies. Be careful when sending emails or copies to many recipients. If they have not given permission for you to broadcast their email address, you might fall foul of the Data Protection Act. You can send the email to yourself, with blind copies to everyone else, but if you do this no one else will know who the other recipients are. The date and time and your email address are automatically entered.

▶ Subject

Write your subject heading carefully so the recipient knows what the email is about and can prioritize when to read it. Use URGENT only when it is really urgent; otherwise it loses its impact.

▶ Design

Some elements of the email can be designed to reflect your image. You could, for example, incorporate your logo at the head of every email, provided it does not take long to download at the other end; if it does, people will not bother with it. It will certainly make your emails more interesting to look at when printed out.

▶ Salutation

Etiquette for email is still developing. The salutation ranges from 'Dear...' (formal), through 'Good morning', or 'Hello' to 'Hi!' (informal). Some people just write the recipient's name. If in doubt, go more formal.

▶ The body of the email

Short emails are no problem, but long emails should be planned, along the same lines as for a letter: introductory paragraph, main points, conclusion – next steps. Do use paragraphs, with spaces between them, they are so much easier to read. Use indented paragraphs for emphasis, and numbering or bullet points if they help the reader. Use subheadings too, if that will help.

Use the spellchecker and punctuate properly, using a capital I and initial capital letters for names. Do not use symbols and smileys unless you know the person well. Do not key in words or sentences in all caps; people think you are shouting at them.

If you are writing about two different subjects to the same person on the same day, send two emails. People often do not read to the bottom of a long email. If a document you refer to or something you want to say is really long, send it as an attachment, even though it takes time to download. If you are forwarding emails, write a short sentence to introduce what you are sending – it focuses the reader's mind.

▶ Sign off

Sign off with 'Regards' or 'Kind regards' if you wish to sound friendly, or 'Yours sincerely' perhaps for a first, formal contact. Add your name, and in many cases your contact details (address and telephone number). These are useful as references, particularly as an email gives no indication of where your business is. You could also add a short tailpiece about what your business does. James, for example, could add: 'Jay's Gardens for all your garden design, landscaping and planting'.

Emails are often, unfortunately, poorly constructed and written because they are fast-food correspondence, but this type of email does little to enhance the image of your business. There are often things you can do to improve your emails.

Remember this: Double check recipients

Be careful when you click on 'Send'. Your email is winging its way to the named recipient(s).

Next time you write a letter or an email, make sure it lives up to your image.

Publicity material

Your image should be carried through into all your advertising and publicity material. Under this heading come many of the things mentioned previously: flyers, posters, business cards, compliments slips. It also includes such things as printed T-shirts, baseball caps, sweatshirts, balloons, umbrellas, key rings and pens – in fact, anything that has your name and logo on it. (Vehicles are dealt with in the next section.)

You have chosen your business name, logo and colours, so you have a good starting point for your material. This is publicity material, so must be eye-catching in either a sober or brash way, or somewhere between the two, depending on your business. When you are next in a building which has small posters, or flyers, showing 'What's On', look at them consciously to see which catches your eye. They will probably be those that are on brightly coloured paper, with only a few words which stand out at a distance. They may have a white background, with bright lettering in a large font size – although just black and white can be very effective. They must be easy to read and convey their message quickly and succinctly; no one is going to stop and read a lot of small print.

TYPES OF PUBLICITY MATERIAL

Think about each of the following as they apply to your business.

▶ **Compliments slips**

These are usually the width of an A4 sheet but not very deep – you can get four out of one A4 portrait sheet. They should be the same colour as your headed paper with your name, logo and contact details laid out to leave enough room for a short, written message. They also need the words 'With compliments' on them somewhere. They are very useful to attach to something you want to post to someone where a covering letter is not necessary.

▶ Business cards

Business cards can be landscape ▭ or portrait ▯. Landscape is more useful, and fits better into business card containers. As well as the name, logo and contact details of your business, they should have your own name, job title and phone number(s). These are personal cards, no bigger than a credit card; if they are too big, they will not fit into other people's card holders. They have the same colours and background as your headed paper, but give a good impression if they are on reasonably thick card. You might have to go to a professional to get these printed.

▶ Leaflets and flyers

Many, if not most, small businesses need leaflets to hand out or leave in display stands. A leaflet gives more information than a poster, which is often for a special event. They are normally on A5 paper, or A4 landscape folded into three and printed double-sided. They need to have the same background colour as your headed paper, particularly if you want them to stand out from the crowd; you may wish to use a really startling colour for a good reason, but consider, as usual, what you want your image to convey.

▶ A5 flyers

Thinking of A5 flyers, you will want the design to catch your readers' eye and lead them through the important information because flyers are used for special events or promotions. Here you have to think of 'eye flow' and 'eye dwell'. Consider this sheet of A5:

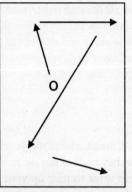

Figure 3.5 How the eyes scan a document

The O in the middle represents the actual centre of the page; this is not where your eye first looks. It looks a little to the left and slightly up from there, at about 11 o'clock. It then travels towards the top left-hand corner, across the top of the page from left to right, diagonally down towards the left-hand corner, a little below the centre circle, and then on a short diagonal to the bottom right-hand corner. Three things follow from this:

1 Headings are usually across the top; put them in the middle or towards the bottom and they will not be so eye-catching.

2 If you want people to do something, put it in the bottom right-hand corner, not the left.

3 The bottom left-hand corner is, therefore, a dead area, where you can put less important information.

4 Look at posters on advertising hoardings and you will see they follow this pattern, with the brand name usually in the right-hand bottom corner. The zigzag will not necessarily be made up of words, but might be a fashion model's limbs. The same applies to flyers and posters.

If you are designing A5 flyers which will be displayed in stands, make sure that the most important piece of information is visible. If the flyers literally stand in an A5 stand, as they do in the reception area of a hotel, you can only see the top half until you take the flyer out of the stand. Also, make sure they are on paper or card stiff enough to stand up and not flop forward over the stand.

Check that you have all the information you need on the flyer, including contact details as appropriate and that everything is correctly spelled. Misspelled words irritate people who know what the correct spelling should be.

▶ A4 leaflet folded

A4 leaflets folded into thirds vertically are very popular. You can get a lot of information on them and they are easy to carry, hand out and store. Consider your target readership and write for them. What will they be looking for in your business? What will make them want to pick up your leaflet? Put that information on the front. As you open the leaflet the next part you read will be the right-hand folded-in part; here expand on your important information on the front. Open the leaflet completely and you now have an A4 landscape sheet on which to put photographs, text, other visuals and all sorts of good information. Fold the sheet up again and turn to the back. This is where you can put all your contact details. (When people pick up a newspaper or any other folded reading matter, they look at the front, then at the back, and then they open it up.)

▶ Posters

These are often large versions of your A5 flyers and can be anything from A4 to very large (double elephant!). The larger they are, the more expensive they will be. Posters are usually for specific events, such as concerts, sales, fairs or circuses. You need several posters posted round your town or village; one really is not enough. A set of A4 or A3 posters together makes quite a good impact. The same design principles apply as for A5 flyers.

READABILITY

One most important part about all publicity material is that it must be readable by a wide range of people. Professional graphic artists are most helpful, in that their creativity can often say in a well-designed graphic or picture more than just words can convey. However, they may tend to get a little carried away and in their enthusiasm design things which are difficult to read. Sometimes the background image is too obtrusive, sometimes the lettering is too small or in a difficult font. Reversing out (white on black instead on black on white) can cause a problem, especially combinations such as yellow on green or blue on red. You just have to keep a graphic artist's feet on the ground!

 Try it now: Design a flyer

Design your own A5 flyer, taking into account all the advice in this chapter. Think of a special event, such as your shop opening, or a special offer of your product or service, and ask:

✷ What do I want my readers to know?

✷ What do I want my readers to do?

✷ How can I best attract their attention?

Premises and vehicles

PREMISES

Chapter 2 dealt with the outside of premises, which naturally affects your image. Perhaps yours is a craft-based business in a craft centre. How do your premises look from the outside? You would not expect craft centres to be all glass and steel, although some may be, but they are usually built of brick and wood which gives a feeling of craftsmanship.

Perhaps your business is a nursery school or a language school. Nursery schools are often housed in village halls, so you, the proprietor, have little say over the building itself. However, as a tenant, you surely have some influence on whether the grass is cut, the windows are clean and there is sufficient outside light on dark days, with reasonable parking arrangements.

Language schools (and theatre schools) are often housed in unprepossessing buildings; these are generally not highly lucrative businesses, and therefore cannot afford the most modern, light, inviting premises. Their customers, students, have little money themselves, but should be taught in as pleasant surroundings as possible. Put yourself in your customers' shoes and see what you can do to improve the outside of your premises (perhaps a coat of paint is all that is needed). It will all help your image.

The inside of your premises is even more important, for that is where you and your clients, if they come to you, will spend most of the working time. Everyone knows, when they think about it, what makes business premises agreeable to work in:

- well-decorated walls, probably in pastel shades
- appropriate floor covering – the carpet can be good, but can you keep it clean?
- good, directional lighting with spotlights and desk lights
- tasteful curtains or blinds
- matching furniture, wherever possible
- attractive, well-crafted pictures on the walls
- plants, if appropriate
- no unnecessary, penetrative noise from outside
- fresh-smelling rooms
- enough storage space
- tidy, well-ordered and clean rooms
- up-to-date IT, wherever possible
- enough space
- a private space, if necessary.

You probably have all these things in your own home. They are equally important in your business premises, whether these premises are actually in your own home or part of an office complex, a workshop, small factory, shop or restaurant. Everything enhances or detracts from your image.

Remember, too, the loos, washbasins, soap dispensers and hand-drying facilities. Do they match up to the rest of the premises? If they do not, do something about it.

Now add the crockery and glassware you use for staff and client refreshments. Mugs or cups? What colour and design? Some designs look good, but are difficult to hold. It is worth spending a little on these items so that the entire image is one of business-like competence, but at the same time welcoming and appropriate to your work.

VEHICLES

Some businesses need vans, trucks or lorries, while others need just a car. You may well have a vehicle to start with, because you have been running a pilot for your business, but sometimes you need to start afresh with good vehicles specifically for work. Obviously, all vehicles need servicing regularly and to be kept in good working order – you cannot work without them. They also need to be kept clean and free from rubbish and un-business-like clutter. Sweet papers, cigarette ends and children's toys do not give a good impression. It is true that in most instances you will not be giving people lifts in your vehicles, but they are likely to see them parked outside their premises, making deliveries or arriving at their home.

Most cars used for business do not have the company name and logo on them, but vans, trucks and lorries often do. This is where your company name, logo and some idea of what you do come in. If you can, choose a vehicle with a colour which will allow your name and logo to show up in the company colours. Your business will have a bearing on how eye-catching your publicity material – for that is what it is – should be. Does it need to be fairly discreet, or definitely shouting that your company, and its vehicles, are in business? Match the advertising on your vehicles with your chosen image.

Local sign-writers will usually do a good job for you; find, if you can, other vehicles they have done and look at the quality of that work. Is the lettering clean and crisp? Have they distorted the logo in any way? Can you still see the pencil lines they have used? Is it correctly spelled? Sign-writers, begging their pardon, are not the best spellers in the world. They usually spell unusual names without any problem, because they pay attention to them, but leaving a letter out of a common word, or reversing two letters, is not unheard of. 'Wocestershire', for someone who lives in that county is a familiar name: too familiar. Did you spot that an 'r' was missing? If the sign-writer has done work on your vehicles, check every detail before you take your vehicles away.

Should you go for new(ish) vehicles or older ones? One thing you do need, above all, is reliability, which predisposes you towards the newer end of the market. Remember that depreciation of your vehicles is an allowance your accountant can make in your annual accounts. So you could go for something smart and up to date. You may wonder if your customers and clients think you should not be driving around in a rather up-market car, but subconsciously they are more likely to be thinking your business is doing well. This may be the time to go for that second car in the household, although you and your domestic partner need to think about carbon footprints and how necessary two cars really are.

Remember this: Insure your vehicles correctly

One final thought about your vehicles, which are very much part of you and your image: vans, lorries and trucks obviously need insurance specifically for them; remember to insure your car for business as well as pleasure.

Personnel

How do you, your partners, your fellow directors and your staff come across to your customers or clients? Do you all look, and sound, business-like but at the same time friendly and approachable?

YOU

You, yourself (along with partners and fellow directors), are the most important person. You set the tone, and how you appear and seem to others will dictate the flavour of your business.

▶ Appearance

First of all, your appearance. What do you, should you, wear on different occasions? The answer is, naturally, whatever is appropriate to the situation and your business. You would not expect an art teacher to appear in a suit in front of a class, but a suit for that same art teacher might be appropriate for visiting the bank. People attending business clubs tend to dress in a business-like manner, whereas members of social clubs are far more informally dressed. Some people are more comfortable in casual dress than in business dress, and vice versa, but there are times to set your own comfort aside and dress as others would expect to see you.

Sometimes uniform is appropriate for everyone working in that particular occupation, and sometimes protective clothing is essential. If you do not wear what is required in these situations, neither will other members of your team.

Businesspeople, particularly women, need to spend time planning their wardrobe. Unless your business happens to be in the fashion industry in some way, you will not be expected to dress in the height of fashion, but neither will your customers or clients wish to see you looking old-fashioned, dowdy and unkempt. That would give quite the wrong impression of your business and your image.

Pay particular attention to your shoes, which should be reasonably up to date, but comfortable, especially if you are on your feet all day. Different shoes, for men and women, make people stand and walk in a different way; actors often begin to build a character starting with the shoes, the feet and the walk: it is difficult to rehearse a period piece in trainers.

What about colour? There are colours which suit you and those which do not. Find out those which do, those which enhance your appearance, and those which make you look less than confident and business-like. Good, well-made clothes, even if they are not very expensive, together with a good hairstyle will help you appear the businessperson you want to be. This goes for men as well as women.

▶ Sound

How do you sound to your customers and clients, both face to face and on the phone? You have already heard yourself on your phone message, but telephones tend to distort voices, so how do you tell how you sound out loud? Recording your voice has the same effect as the telephone, unless you are recorded by someone who knows what they are doing and has the right recording equipment.

The only way you can really tell how you are being received by others is to watch their reactions. Even if you have to convey bad news, it can be done in a positive way, and the other person's reactions will tell you how well you have succeeded in maintaining or building your customer relations.

YOUR PARTNERS AND FELLOW DIRECTORS

Everyone is different and will approach the business in a slightly different way. Indeed, this can be a great strength, if each member of the team is allowed and encouraged to use their particular talents to the full. Sometimes your partners or fellow directors can be brusque, which may or may not matter. If that person is tied to a computer all day, perhaps it does not, but their manner can still create an unhelpful atmosphere in the workplace. Somehow, if the problem is affecting the business, it must be tackled before it goes too far, and only you and other team members will have a feeling for how best to do this.

When there are several of you running the business, agreement on dress code and customer service policy is even more important. Regular team meetings can often deal with small problems before they become large ones.

One very practical thing you can do if several of you are out and about a great deal is to set up, electronically or manually, a central system for keeping a log of messages. A manual log would look something like this:

MESSAGE LOG

Date	Time	Message for	Message from	Message	Dealt with (tick when done)
24/3	10.30	RB	Cantabile	Can you contact Peter on 324792?	

It is easier for someone to check the log than to rely on messages on scraps of paper or Post-it notes. It also means other members of the team will see the messages and can add further information, or deal with the message in your absence if necessary.

Teamwork is the name of the game.

YOUR STAFF

All these things apply to your staff, even if it is only one part-time person. Their appearance, the way they sound and how well they stick to agreed customer service policy are all just as important for them as for you. However, staff, particularly new members of staff, need guidelines to follow and often training in customer service. Imagine, if this is your first job after leaving school, how you will feel in the new world of work. There is so much to learn and so many situations to cope with. Experienced staff do have the experience, but can become set in their ways, but they can change their routines and behaviour if necessary. It is unwise to think that very mature people cannot change – they can, if properly dealt with and consulted and their strengths used.

It is up to you to show by example and to develop your staff to reach the agreed standards. This all takes time, but it is time well invested. Nobody ever said that starting your own small business was easy!

POLICY

Everyone is aware that good customer service can make or break a business. You remember the outstanding service and the bad experiences, which you are likely to relate to other people. Your clients or customers do the same thing.

You and your team need to be consistent, so a customer service policy is helpful. For example, how many times do you allow the telephone to ring before answering it? What is your policy on complaints and returns? How will you deal with an angry customer when other people are near? The answer is to ask the customer to move to a quiet place away from the others, so a policy as to where that place is will help you all to know exactly what to do.

Only you know the circumstances likely to arise in your business, so establish guidelines for dealing with them; these guidelines are best established after consultation with your team, who are your 'internal' customers. If you are on your own, you can do what you think best.

Try it now: Customer service policy

Whether you are working on your own or with a team, draw up preliminary guidelines for the following:
* dress code
* answering the phone
* message taking
* dealing with complaints
* dealing with returns, if appropriate.

Remember this: People first

People are the most important part of any business. A truism, but true.

Focus points

* Your business image is beginning to emerge and is conveyed by your name and logo, your stationery design, your publicity material and your personal image.
* What will your customers and clients deduce from your image?
* One final thought: satisfy yourself that subcontractors and associates work to your standards of competence and customer service.

Next step

Now you are ready to market your business, to let people know you have arrived. Chapter 4 goes into detail about your marketing strategies, where you advertise, if at all, how to get the best out of networking meetings and how to make a presentation to your customers or clients.

Marketing

In this chapter you will learn:

- ► *How to write and design effective marketing materials including leaflets, flyers, brochures, posters and mailshots*
- ► *How to choose the right social media marketing tools*
- ► *How to use advertising to promote your business*
- ► *How to set up, design and manage a business website*
- ► *How to network and make a short presentation*
- ► *How to manage a stall at a trade fair or similar event.*

Marketing your business is about attracting customers and clients to your new business, letting them know you have arrived, and then keeping in touch with them, keeping your name constantly before them and updating them on anything new. There is a variety of marketing tools you can use, so this chapter leads you through the advantages and disadvantages of each, reminds you of some of the design and layout features you tried out in Chapter 3, and gives advice on the content and distribution of leaflets, flyers, brochures, mailshots, your website and advertising; it also gives hints and tips about trade shows, networking and digital marketing.

Self-assessment: What do you know about marketing?

By the time you have worked through this chapter you will be able to answer all the following questions. How many can you answer now?

1 What is the main purpose of a leaflet?

2 What is the main purpose of a flyer?

3 What is the main purpose of a brochure or catalogue?

4 What are the two main types of mailshot?

5 What should the homepage of your website contain?

6 What does AIDA stand for?

7 What sort of business should attend trade shows and exhibitions?

8 Where is your nearest and most appropriate networking group?

9 What should you wear when making a public presentation of your product or service?

10 How do you overcome nerves?

11 Which digital marketing platform is best for your business?

Leaflets, flyers, brochures and mailshots

What is the difference between a leaflet, a flyer and a brochure? **Leaflets** tend to be general, telling people about various aspects of your business. They contain more information than flyers, so are often an A4 folded in thirds, or an A5 booklet of a few pages. **Flyers** are used more for special events – perhaps a sale coming up, or an exhibition; more often than not they are on a single sheet of A5.

Brochures are more hefty and go into much more detail than leaflets; they often have examples and photographs of products or services and information about the key people in the business. If you think of a theatre or concert hall, a brochure will give details of events for the next six months; these are supported by leaflets giving details of specific events and then, perhaps nearer the time, flyers to promote events they feel they need to push. Brochures can be thought of as mini catalogues, where the whole range of products is fully described, with order forms and price lists.

Another way of looking at how these three items differ is: your website is your leaflet, giving general information about your business; the different web pages give details about the various aspects of your business, with links through to product descriptions – your brochure or catalogue in effect; stop press items or eye-catching ads on the home page are your flyers, attracting attention to specific promotions or events.

Your clients or customers will always want to know how much you charge. It is better to have separate price lists to accompany leaflets, which you do not want to have reprinted too often. Catalogues, brochures and flyers usually contain all the necessary information, including prices (and postage and packing, if appropriate). It is much easier to change details such as prices on the Web, but it is unwise to do it too frequently and without warning. Special promotions usually have a set date when they will finish. If you change prices frequently, you need a foolproof ordering system so that you do not charge customers the wrong amount.

Most businesses need leaflets and a website. Some need digital marketing, brochures and catalogues, both printed and electronic, and many need flyers to boost their marketing campaigns. Sometimes leaflets and flyers are interchangeable or complementary; on an exhibition stand you will often see both the general information (leaflets) and specific information (flyers). Sometimes there are brochures or catalogues as well, depending on your type of business. See later in this chapter for digital marketing hints and tips.

Mailshots can be a good way of marketing your business and distributing leaflets, flyers and brochures. We will look at mailshots a little later in this chapter.

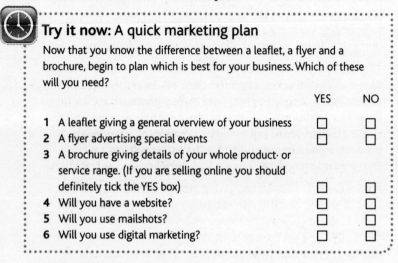

Try it now: A quick marketing plan

Now that you know the difference between a leaflet, a flyer and a brochure, begin to plan which is best for your business. Which of these will you need?

	YES	NO
1 A leaflet giving a general overview of your business	☐	☐
2 A flyer advertising special events	☐	☐
3 A brochure giving details of your whole product· or service range. (If you are selling online you should definitely tick the YES box)	☐	☐
4 Will you have a website?	☐	☐
5 Will you use mailshots?	☐	☐
6 Will you use digital marketing?	☐	☐

LEAFLETS

A little more detail, now, about each marketing tool, starting with leaflets. Let's start with the format, because the format will dictate the amount of material you can include. A4 folded, double-sided, can easily be done on your home computer if you have the skill and a good printer, especially for colour. Small booklets, probably A5, are more complicated, because of getting the pages in the right order, and possibly stapled down the central spine. In Chapter 3 you practised designing a flyer, so carry these thoughts into a leaflet and decide the type and amount of information you want to include. In Chapter 1 you defined your product or service, your potential customers or clients and your competition. Bearing these things in mind, ask yourself: What basic information will my customers or clients need?

This will vary considerably, depending on your type of business, but will probably include the range of your products or services, some indication of who these products or services are suitable for, the main selling points and often your location. Remember to include contact details, opening times if appropriate and, in some cases, a small local map.

You will already have chosen your font, or fonts, in Chapter 3, so use these to their best advantage. Increase the print size where appropriate and think about spacing and 'white space'. Spacing is the space between lines of print, and white space is the space surrounding the text or graphics. Leave plenty of white space so that your important information stands out; crowded pages do not attract the reader.

For descriptive text use short sentences, 15–20 words average, and write in plain, simple English, with correct grammar and spelling. To attract attention use questions, provided you do not give your readers the chance to say 'no'. For example, a question which starts 'Are you interested in…?' allows the reader to say 'no'. One reader lost straight away. Much better to ask an intriguing question like 'How many times have you…?' Quite often in a leaflet, direct, easily understood information is all that is needed. Do not use long words which people do not understand, although technical terms are fine for technical readers.

You can design your leaflets yourself, or go to a graphic designer and copywriter to do it for you. These people are professionals, so will charge you accordingly, but it might be worthwhile if you or your team do not have the time or the skills. In all cases, the final proofreading (literally finding mistakes in the phone numbers, names and so on) is down to you. If your spelling and grammar are a bit suspect, this, too, is where you may need help. Consider attracting attention by using graphics, drawings, photographs or even cartoons which reflect your image and the products or services you are offering. Do not infringe other people's copyright by using their material without permission.

You will probably want a substantial run of leaflets, say 1,000 to begin with. It sounds a lot, but you can soon get through them. Send your copy to the printer down the line or on disk, but let your printer have a hard copy as well. Your colours may not be as vibrant as the final version will be, but a master copy gives a good idea of what the final print should look like. Choose an appropriate weight of paper (your printer will advise you) and avoid anything too glossy, which catches the light and can be difficult to read. Save the glossy paper for the brochures and catalogues. Once the printer has your copy on their computer, it is very easy for them to make amendments and print off further copies, so additional print runs should not be too expensive. Given the right skills and equipment, you can produce your own leaflets, so you will not need to print so many at a time.

Try it now: Create a leaflet

In Chapter 3 you designed a flyer for a special event. Now create a leaflet for your business, on A4 landscape folded in three and printed on both sides. Chapter 3 (publicity material) gives advice on what to put where; now add the text, graphics, photos and anything else which will help convey your message about your business.

When you are happy with the final draft, try it on friends, family and business colleagues and contacts before sending the final, final version to the printers. If you do not have the computer skills to create your leaflet yourself, make a rough draft by hand.

FLYERS

Flyers are good for special events or one-off promotions. They are sometimes preferable to leaflets for businesses where you go to other people and work in their homes because they can easily be distributed and are less expensive than leaflets. So flyers have many uses.

Flyers are, above all, to attract attention, particularly to something new or something exciting. They are usually on one side of A5 and are colourful and eye-catching, as you saw in Chapter 3, where you thought about their design and designed your own for a special event.

Colourful paper or card attracts attention, but so do the words on flyers. Certain words are more attractive than others, literally enticing people to read them. These include FREE, NEW, NOW, YOU, SPECIAL and, interestingly, PROVEN. 'Proven' is a surprise in this list, but when you watch television ads, count how many times 'proven' appears in ads which promote something vaguely scientific or clinical, such as 'proven whiteness' or 'proven to reduce the appearance of...' So, if your business is medically or scientifically based, even basically, 'proven' might be a good word to attract your clients – but you should be able to substantiate it. People are aware that the other words are there to hook them in, but they still read them. This is the secret of a good flyer – it hooks people in. Notice that the above are all fairly short words.

Next time you see an A5 flyer which hooks you in to read it, analyse what it is which attracted you. Some colours are so bright, they repel, and might not match your image. The same flyer, in a variety of colours, spread out on a display table can be very eye-catching.

When you spread out your flyers for display, as opposed to handing them out or doing leaflet drops, fan them out and do not make neat piles. People do not like to disturb something that looks too tidy. If you are building a display of cans in a supermarket, you remove at least one can so that shoppers do not have to start disturbing the display themselves. If you are handing out flyers, or any other kind of handout, fan these out, too: it is just easier to hand out one at a time.

BROCHURES

Brochures (and catalogues) are much more substantial and detailed. They are long-term marketing tools, which you should not need to have printed too often. If your business depends on the seasons, then four editions a year are usually enough, with perhaps extra flyers or even leaflets for sale times.

Brochures can be any size, depending on the information you want to put in them, but are normally A5 landscape or portrait, or A4 portrait. Their covers are often glossy, sometimes glitzy, although craft-based businesses tend to use eco-friendly, rougher paper which gives an impression of nature and earthiness.

They are good for network marketing businesses and those which sell through the post; they can also be good as backup for those who sell, or advertise, online. Brochures give people time to browse, think and choose exactly what they want. Buyers need to see colour, know size details, what items are made of, price, delivery details and how to order. Photographs need to be top quality, so unless photography is your own business or hobby it is best to employ a professional photographer who specializes in 'commercial' photography. It follows that they are expensive to produce, but might be the best marketing tool for your business.

Incidentally, you do not have to put plastic sleeves round brochures when sending them by post, provided the recipient's name and address are quite clear. You do risk their being damaged, of course.

> **Remember this:** Get the most out of a flyer
>
> You can use the back of a flyer to market the whole range of your products or services. Remember to include your contact details.

Your business will probably benefit from using leaflets, flyers or brochures, or a combination of these tools. Almost all businesses will find it profitable, in the end, to use one of these. Mailshots, on the other hand, are better for some types of business than others.

MAILSHOTS

Being on the receiving end of mailshots, you could be forgiven for thinking they are the most effective form of advertising known, since everyone seems to use them. But consider for a moment how many you, personally, have responded to; probably only a very few. This is the big minus for this form of advertising – the response rate is traditionally low, and yet it remains a much-used method.

Mailshots can be selective or non-selective. Selective mailshots are particularly good for business-to-business trading, for a consultant or a tool manufacturer, for example. Unless you intend to send mailshots in very large numbers, it would be advisable to use selective mailshots to specified target groups. This could be approached in several ways, for instance alphabetical, geographical. Try to compile as big a list as possible of organizations which might use your product or service. List the most obvious ones first, but do not be too rigid, particularly if you are offering products or services which might have a more universal application. Think of organizations which, although they might be diverse in themselves, have a common need which is covered by your product or service.

Ask yourself: How many products do I have and does this affect how many potential customers are available for my business?

When you have compiled your list, rather than tackle it all in one go, work through it piecemeal and select a manageable number: this will help you to regulate the time involved in preparation, follow-up and evaluating the results. This does not mean to say that you only need to prepare the number of mailshots you actually plan to send out. If you have a period of time in which you can make up a large number of packs, by all means do so. You do not necessarily have to despatch them all at the same time.

As a rule of thumb, aim to send each mailshot to a named person. This may involve a telephone call to find out from a business who is responsible for your product or service. Obtain:

► the name and job title

► the correct name of the company

► the full postal address.

You cannot always rely on trade directory information, even in the current edition, because people move or change jobs and businesses get taken over; it is best to check.

The mailshot package itself will probably consist of a brochure or some other form of printed matter describing your product or service, together with a standard letter of introduction. Follow the KISS principle and Keep It Short and Simple. Do not be tempted to tell the recipients your whole story at this first encounter – but just enough for them to want to know more.

Try to keep your letter to one side of one sheet of headed paper. Follow this broad format: introduce yourself and your organization by stating who you are and what you are offering, and in effect ask 'Can we do business?' Indicate that you intend to follow up this written introduction with a telephone call.

In the letter, do not quote a precise time when you will ring (something may prevent you) or suggest a specific date for a meeting (you do not know the recipient's commitments), but wait until you telephone, when you will have a direct response to a suggested date, and alternatives can be discussed – and resolved – there and then.

Set yourself a deadline, and some sort of timetable for your telephone follow-up calls. Probably the best times, from the recipients' point of view, are Tuesday to Thursday, preferably mornings if you can make it. Monday mornings and Friday afternoons are probably best avoided – the recipients are just getting their week underway on the one, and thinking about going off on the other. There might well be cases, of course, where these are the ideal times to telephone. You will get to know your own type of business best.

Preparation for your follow-up telephone call will help it to be effective. Compile a checklist of points to make. Try to avoid a fully written-out script. You can be thrown if the recipient does not respond in the way you expect – or asks a question at the wrong time!

Your call could take this form, once you are connected to the right person:

1 Identify yourself and your organization.

2 Ask whether your brochure has been received, to which the answer will broadly be 'yes' or 'no'.

3 If the answer is 'no', briefly explain the substance of your letter and brochure in broad terms (having a copy of both in front of you will prove invaluable in these circumstances).

4 Offer to send a further set.

5 At this stage, and if the answer to your original question was 'yes', ask whether your kind of product or type of service is being stocked or used at present. Again the answer will broadly be 'yes' or 'no'.

6 This is your cue to describe the benefits to that business of what you are offering: in the case of the 'no' answer you can start from basics; with the 'yes' response, explain what is different about yours, and the benefits to that business of including your product or service in their existing range.

7   If at this stage there are discernible signs of interest, try to gain a definite commitment of some sort, e.g. a meeting, or even a sample order.

8   Be sure to confirm any arrangements in writing, and ensure that they are met in full.

9   If, however, the response is still negative, ask whether there is any possibility of reconsidering in the future, and whether you may ring again.

It might be worthwhile sending a letter thanking the individual for the conversation, and confirming that you will be in touch in a few months. File the information for future reference – and mark your diary to remind you to make that call when the time comes.

▶ Layout

When writing your mailshot, whether it is hard copy or electronic, take these points into consideration:

▶ The heading should be large and bold enough to attract attention, centred, above the 'Dear…'

▶ Use hooks in the heading, such as the words listed in the section on 'Flyers and brochures' above. SAVE is another hook word.

▶ Sign the letters personally, if you can.

▶ Put at least one, possibly two PSs after your signature. People look first at who the letter is to, which makes them glance at the heading. Then they look at who it is from, so they read a PS before they read the body of the letter. Put your main message there.

▶ If you are enclosing a glossy brochure and need to clip the letter to it, use a coated paper clip, so as not to damage the glossy paper.

▶ Stuff the envelope so that the reader sees immediately, when opening it, the important paper(s) you want them to see.

HPZ

Helen's Party Zone

21 Stevenage Road
Amberfield Rutland
RP10 2JL
Tel: 01624 324729
Fax: 01624 359705
e-mail: hpz@aol.com
www.hpz.net

September 2015

Mrs Alice Humberton
128 Medcroft Road
Amberfield
Rutland
RP11 3BR

NEW for this season

Dear Mrs Humberton

With Halloween and Christmas coming up, you'll be thinking about parties for your family and friends, particularly the children. So what's new for this season? Visit our showroom to

- Hear the special Halloween ghost noise CD

- See the sparkly new Christmas decorations

- Feel the soft touch of our luxury washable table runners to enhance your dinner table

I believe you were delighted with our party products last year, so I look forward to seeing you again soon.

With kind regards

Helen

Helen Howard

PS. Don't miss our SPECIAL OFFER Halloween masks for your children's party.

VAT Registration No: 765 2108 76   Sole proprietor: Helen Howard

Figure 4.1 Example mailshot letter

Figure 4.1 is an example of a mailshot letter from the proprietor of a party provision business to one of her regular customers.

Your website and digital marketing

Almost all businesses need a website, to be seen to be up to date and to display their products or services to sell, whether online or in some other way. A website increases the potential customer base enormously, allowing you to sell worldwide if you wish.

WEBSITE DESIGN

It is important that your website is professionally designed by someone who knows what they are doing. If your business is computers, your customers may well expect you to be able to design and maintain your own website, but most people starting in business will need the expertise of a professional. Most colleges run courses on website design, which is helpful if you are setting up a website for a local club or society, perhaps. Professional website designers will probably advertise in directories, or online or through networking. Personal recommendation is often the best.

Your designer will need to know your purpose in having a website. Is it to sell online, to give information and contact details about your product or service, or to demonstrate, through animation, what you can do for your clients? For example, a garden landscape designer may wish to conduct you round a garden he or she has designed.

Websites usually start with a home page, giving a broad view of your business, and leading your customers into the other pages. It is important that the site is well designed so that potential customers who enter your website can find what they want quickly: if they struggle, they will probably give up. If you are selling online (e-commerce), you will need a good customer ordering system. For selling techniques on the Internet, see Chapter 5.

▶ To start

You will need:

- ▶ A modem or router, linking you to the Internet. These are integral to most modern systems.

- ▶ An ISP (Internet Service Provider), such as BT, Virgin, etc.

- ▶ A domain name – the name a website visitor keys in to enter your website. This should be as short and simple as possible, incorporating your business name. Your website designer will advise you on all these things.

▶ Broadband

Broadband is a package which allows you to upload and download files and graphics far more quickly than the original 'standard' method of transmitting information. If you are likely to transmit or receive long documents, complicated graphics and/or photographs, broadband is highly desirable. For animation it is essential. You pay for the level of service you need. Again, your website designer will advise you.

▶ Website maintenance

Once your site is designed and up and running, you must make arrangements to maintain it, keeping it up to date, making sure your ordering and payment systems for your products (if you are selling online) are working efficiently and providing you with the statistics you need to monitor your site's efficiency. For simple systems, or if you are computer literate, you could do this yourself, but most businesses rely on their website designer to provide this service. They cannot give you good service unless you feed them the appropriate information daily, weekly, monthly, or as and when, according to your business. There is nothing more off-putting to a potential customer than a website which is out of date or says 'Data not available'.

▶ Security

You hear horror stories of viruses, worms and unwanted spam; all these things can happen to you. You should consider an ISP which provides spam filters, parental control (if necessary), a firewall, virus protection, spyware protection and antivirus software, etc.

▶ **Costs**

You will need to pay for:

▶ A phone line (for most applications). Broadband allows you to use the same line for Internet transmissions and phone calls simultaneously. You could consider having a dedicated phone line for business purposes if you work from home, which makes it easier to separate your business phone calls from your personal calls for bookkeeping purposes.

▶ The services of your ISP, probably monthly

▶ Your domain name, probably annually

▶ Your website design

▶ Your website maintenance

Try it now: Setting up your website

Answer these questions to help you make decisions about your website:

		YES	NO
1	Are you ready to set up your website now? (If you are selling online the answer must be 'yes'.)	☐	☐
2	Do you have the necessary hardware and software?	☐	☐
3	Does this include security provision?	☐	☐
4	Are you skilled enough to design your own website?	☐	☐
5	Are you clear about what you want your website to do?	☐	☐
6	Have you decided on your hook words for search engine optimization?	☐	☐
7	Will you or a member of your team maintain your website?	☐	☐

If you have answered 'no' to any of these questions, you know which areas you have to tackle. If you have answered 'no' to all of them, you are probably not ready to set up your website – yet.

As you can see, the cost of a good website can be considerable, and must be taken into account when forming and using your business plan and the cost of your overheads. It is probably wise not to embark on a website too early in your business life, unless you intend to sell exclusively online. Get your business off the ground first, particularly if you are manufacturing products, so that you are confident you have plenty of stock to sell. Service providers can afford to start a little earlier.

SOCIAL MEDIA MARKETING

Social media marketing, or digital marketing, is a must for many small businesses. Personal recommendation is often one of the best ways of expanding your business or service; marketing messages sent to your existing customer base using digital marketing tools can very quickly reach a much greater potential customer base than using more conventional marketing materials, although these still have their place. It is almost as if you were communicating with your future clients or customers face to face. Your messages could go viral!

Before you decide which digital marketing tool is right for you, you need to revisit your marketing plan and probably change or expand it to incorporate your digital marketing strategy. Ask yourself these questions:

▶ Is my current marketing plan bringing me closer to my desired goals?

▶ In what ways can social media further my marketing efforts?

▶ What do I want to achieve with social media marketing?

▶ Who am I trying to reach?

▶ Do I know where they are on the web?

These five questions are taken from Teach Yourself *Social Media Marketing* by Nick Smith, a digital marketing expert. Nick sets out very clearly what you should consider when making your plan and goes on to describe, in detail, how to get started on Facebook, Twitter etc. and how best to use these tools for your own marketing. It is an excellent book and great value for money, but bear in mind that it is written for the American market so not all the statistics and platforms mentioned are necessarily applicable to the UK.

Here we will summarize the main points you need to take into account when making your own social media marketing decisions.

▶ Your social media marketing plan

The two most important of the five questions mentioned above are:

▶ What are your main digital marketing goals?

▶ Which customers or clients will you be targeting and how do you know where they are on the web?

You might well start with Facebook or LinkedIn, but there are many other platforms you could use. Make sure that whichever platforms you use, there must be a link back to your website.

Remember this: Get connected
Social media marketing is about getting close to your customers or clients. Your website is where you sell your products or services.

▶ Social media marketing platforms

▶ **Facebook** Create a personal profile and a business page, showing photos, sales information, special offers and so on. You need a mix of different types of content and you can include short videos and music if appropriate. Images of hairstyles or gardens say so much more than just words.

▶ **Twitter** Although messages are limited to 140 characters, Twitter users devour these messages daily. You can speedily reach hundreds, if not thousands, of potential clients or customers with news of your very latest special offers or an invitation to your next exhibition. Tweets are a bit like flyers.

▶ **LinkedIn** Best for business-to-business customers or clients. It is similar to Facebook but business orientated. Like Facebook, you should have a personal profile and a business page. This should be a concise explanation of who you are, what you do and why other businesses should do business with you.

▶ **Blogs** These are usually free to set up and are often part of your business website. Blogs should be your company's online marketing nerve centre, with links to your other social media marketing platforms. You will need a blogging platform on your website, perhaps using WordPress. Nick Smith's book goes into great detail of how to set up your blog. Your blog must be updated regularly.

▶ **YouTube** Has a Get Started page to take you through the set up process, very similar to Facebook and Twitter. Use it for your promotional or descriptive videos and embed them into your Facebook and blog pages.

For all these platforms know your customers or clients, what they want and where they are likely to look for it. Use all the marketing techniques you know to get the right messages to the right people.

Try it now

1 Write your social media marketing plan – what are your goals and who are you targeting?
2 Decide which platform(s) you are going to start with, probably Facebook or LinkedIn.
3 Set up your own account for your chosen platform(s).
4 Get help and advice if you need it.

Case study: Choosing the right channels

In our theatre company, we perform mostly to elderly audiences in clubs and societies. We recently did a very limited straw poll of how many audience members were on Facebook or Twitter. The answer was almost none! So we decided that social media marketing is not necessary to our very small business.

Advertising

CONTENT

Advertisements, like mailshots, can be divided into two categories, selective and non-selective.

1 With **selective advertisements** you will be aiming your material at particular groups or categories of potential customer. One advantage of selective advertising is that you can be very precise in your material, perhaps even to the extent of incorporating jargon, since your target audience will understand. It might also create a (subconscious) impression on the readers that you know what you are talking about – which, of course, you do.

2 **Non-selective advertising** on the other hand, by its very nature, must be more general in its approach, striking a balance between being too basic or elementary for those in the know, and inviting the person who is unfamiliar with the subject to find out more.

This leads us neatly into the well-used advertising formula AIDA – which is particularly applicable to non-selective advertising, for what AIDA aims to do, through the advertising material is to:

▶ gain the **A**ttention of the reader

▶ hold the **I**nterest of the reader

▶ create a **D**esire in the reader for your product or service

▶ stimulate **A**ction in the reader to BUY.

This, after all, is the sole purpose of advertisements. It is the route toward this target which needs careful planning. Let's go through each of these objectives in a little more detail:

▶ Gain the Attention of the reader

As with flyers, you need to lead the reader in to your advertisement, so the list of hook words applies here. These are, once again, FREE, NOW, SAVE, NEW, YOU, SPECIAL and PROVEN. The word SEX is also a hook, or SEXY, but that may not apply to your business. One shop has a hook in its name; it sells up-market, designer handbags, shoes and accessories, and is called 'At Last'.

▶ Hold the Interest of the reader

What is it you are advertising? Something SPECIAL for Christmas, which is a 'must have', particularly for the children or grandchildren? Perhaps it is that NEW accessory for the spring fashions, or that quality bathroom suite which is affordable and can be quickly installed.

▶ Create a Desire in the reader

This is easier if you have written the first two elements well. Perhaps this is the launch of your new business, and they can be one of the first customers to try out your product or service. Perhaps your lawn can at last be free of weeds, or your garden contain a wild section or a pond to help the environment. Chapter 5 – Selling – states that people buy benefits (what is in it for them) not features (facts). Think of how your product or service will benefit your readers.

▶ Stimulate Action in the reader

A reader has to come to you, so you must stimulate action. Tell them to call NOW for a brochure, or visit your website, or be one of your first customers to receive a FREE…

So much for the content of your message, but it will not succeed without good design and layout.

DESIGN AND LAYOUT

All the advice given about design, colour, readable fonts and the design of flyers is relevant to advertisements as well. Here you must also consider the size of the advertisement, and its cost, because that will dictate how much, or how little, you can put in it and therefore its design and layout. You will probably not have as much room as in a flyer, but you still need plenty of white space.

What you are advertising must be clear, eye-catching and specific. Centring everything can work well, although this does not follow the Z formation we looked at in Chapter 3. If you are centring, keep the lines short: you need to lead your reader's eye from one line to the next. If you are using photographs or other illustrations, keep them simple and easy to understand.

Make the call to action clear. Embolden it or put it towards the right-hand bottom corner if you are using the Z formation. Readers need to know exactly what they have to do and they will not spend time searching for it.

Proofreading is always your responsibility. Check and recheck every word, and ask someone else to do it as well. Particularly check familiar things, such as your telephone number or website address. Check, too, that Saturday really is the 16th and not the 17th. Check the headline or main hook, which is probably in larger lettering and you tend to overlook it. Conversely, check the little words such as you/your, an/and, and from/form. These are common errors which the spellchecker will not pick up.

DISTRIBUTION

Advertisements for small businesses usually appear in local newspapers, trade magazines, concert programmes, parish magazines and in shop windows. Advertising in national newspapers is extremely expensive, and at this stage you need not think about advertising on television, but local radio could be a good medium.

One-off advertisements are normally ineffective: you need a short series so that your message is reinforced every time your reader or radio listeners buy a paper or tune in to that station. It can be very useful to get your ad into a special feature in the local newspaper. Perhaps they are having a push on weddings, or local eating establishments; spring is the time for new fashions or gardening. The advertising department of your local newspaper or freebie (which is full of ads) will advise you of future themes or special promotions, when you can usually get a discount.

You will be charged according to the size of your advert and where it appears in the newspaper. Readers read the front page first and then turn to the back page. They read right-hand pages before they read left-hand pages, so, considering the

Z formation, do not let an advertising department sell you space in the bottom left-hand corner of page 2, unless you pay a good deal less for it. The same applies to parish magazines, trade magazines and similar publications.

Postcards in windows are there for a set amount of time and are charged, usually, per week, so you can choose for how long your advertisement appears. If the shop forgets to take it down when the period expires, that is a bonus, unless you have a special offer with a limited timeframe.

Once your business is established you might consider advertising in *Yellow Pages* or in *Yell.com*, or in your *Thomson Local* (www.thomsonlocal.com). These are non-specific, general advertisements, but are widely used, especially for many home services.

Advertisements are a good form of marketing every now and again. Networking is just as good, if not better, particularly when you are very first starting up.

Networking

NETWORKING GROUPS
Networking is one of the most important marketing activities for your small business in the very early days for making contact with potential customers, clients and sometimes suppliers. Most professions have a central organization with local branch meetings you can attend, and they usually welcome visitors from outside their own discipline. For example, the Chartered Institute of Marketing crosses all areas of business and does not cater only for PR specialists. You can learn a great deal from this type of meeting and make useful contacts at the same time.

You can also attend meetings specific to your particular line of business, and indeed need to attend courses to earn points for your Continued Professional Development (CPD), where you can use the breaks to do some very useful networking. For a wider range of small businesses local business clubs can be found all over the UK. Some are locally run, such as breakfast clubs or women in business clubs. Some have a national and international profile, such as Business Network International (BNI). The Federation of Small Businesses also has local branches nationwide.

You can find details of all these institutions, clubs and societies from your local library and on the Internet. The local Chamber of Commerce should also be a good source of information.

▶ Preparation

As with any other business meeting, preparation pays off. You know the name of the contact person and the date, time and venue of the meeting; it is better to make contact and book yourself in, rather than just turn up, particularly if refreshments or breakfast or dinner are involved. If you are being taken as a guest, you may wish to offer to pay for your own attendance, rather than assume that your host will pay for you. Find out the name of the chair or president of the meeting so that you seem knowledgeable when introduced.

Take your marketing material with you – flyers, business cards, leaflets, brochures – anything you think you might need. Have your business cards handy, in a pocket or somewhere else easily accessible. Delving into a briefcase or handbag does not look very organized. Collect other people's business cards, if offered, and take a moment or two to read them; write on the back where and when you met that person. The collection could be the start of your marketing database and it sounds or looks business-like if, when making contact later, you are able to refer to where you first met.

Think about what to wear: business dress is appropriate, depending on what your business is. For some businesses a suit, collar and tie are appropriate, although ties are worn less and less; for others smart casual is the thing to wear. It is easier for women, but a jacket always looks smart and business-like. Women should think about their shoes, too: different shoes make you stand and walk differently and should be in keeping with your general image. If you sell clothes, both men and women can wear the clothes they sell, if they suit them.

Set yourself targets for what you want to achieve at the meeting. It could be one or two good leads, or particular suppliers you want to meet, or people with a particular expertise. Target setting is a good discipline for any business meeting, and networking is no exception.

Try it now: Plan your first networking meeting

The following table might be useful when preparing for your first networking meeting:

NETWORKING MEETING
Contact details
Date, time and venue
Name of chair/president
Materials to take
What to wear
Targets

▶ Make contact

If you have been invited as a guest, your host will probably have arranged to meet you there and be on the lookout for you when you arrive. Nevertheless, you may well arrive on your own, not knowing anyone. Arrive about ten minutes before the meeting is due to start, not too early, when people are still setting up, and certainly not late.

If you are nervous, and some people are, pause outside the door and, in private, take a few really deep breaths. That helps lower your blood pressure and steady your nerves. Then walk in as though you mean it. Walk tall. Do not lurk in the doorway. Look for the person who has the list of attendees and attach your name badge, if there is one, on your lapel, or where other people can see it. This is often easier for men than for women.

Seek out the organizer (probably your original contact) and make yourself known. Groups like to have new members and you will probably be made very welcome. Perhaps they will introduce you to someone who can show you the ropes or your host will be on hand to welcome you and introduce you to other members.

▶ Circulate

Business networking meetings in general usually have two prime objectives:

1 To enable their members to learn through speakers, workshops and so on.

2 To enable their members to get to know each other.

The latter is usually done before the official business of the meeting, or during refreshments and breaks, except where the meeting itself is designated as a networking evening.

If you are on your own, approach a pair or small group, or someone on their own and introduce yourself. This can be quite scary for someone who is not used to putting themselves forward, but it is your business, not yourself, you are promoting and if you truly believe in it, you will not find it so difficult to be proactive in these circumstances. Shake hands and introduce yourself clearly and try to remember the name(s) of the people to whom you are speaking. Their name badges help here. To get the conversation going, ask something like 'How's business?' or 'What's your line of business?' Having listened to them, you will be able to start talking about your own exciting, new business. Be enthusiastic about it, not diffident.

Then repeat the process with other people. You should work the room, talking to more than one or two, unless you find a really good lead you want to pursue. If the meeting is one where you sit down to a meal, or just for a speaker, sit next to someone different and start the introductory process all over again, without being too overwhelming and pushy. Be prepared to hand out your marketing material as appropriate, and have a small notebook handy to jot down details of any contacts you want to follow up.

When the meeting is over, do the usual courteous things like thanking the chair or president, and your host if you have one. Be seen to collect the meeting's own publicity material, even if you have not made up your mind to join, and leave without lingering. Someone has to clear away.

▶ Follow-up

Within the next 48 hours follow up anyone you have promised to contact – phone, text, email, or write and send literature, as agreed. It looks efficient to do this very promptly. Sort out the business cards you have collected and file them in a photograph album or something similar so you can easily find them again. Add the contact details to your database.

Then review the meeting and decide whether you achieved your targets. If not, why not? Was it the wrong sort of meeting for you? Did you stay too long with one person? Did you talk too little, or too much? Look back at your targets for that meeting and write beside each target the outcome of the meeting. If you write these things down, on paper or on the computer, it helps focus your thoughts on what went right and what did not.

TRADE SHOWS AND EXHIBITIONS

Trade shows, exhibitions and local markets are a good way of networking and particularly good for craft-based businesses. Business-to-business shows give good publicity to consultants and manufacturing businesses. A small business will not normally want to take a stand at a large national or international trade show, which is expensive. However, you should consider attending local shows, agricultural fairs and smaller trade shows or exhibitions.

Visit these when you are planning your enterprise, to see if they would be suitable when you are ready for your launch or expansion. If your business is craft-based, you should aim to take part in these shows a couple of times a year. Trade magazines will tell you how to enter.

▶ Booking

You may have to book your space or your stand many months in advance. When booking, make sure you know the answers to these points:

- ▶ the contact to deal with personally – someone you can get to know and build a relationship with

- ▶ confirmation of the dates of your booking

- what times the show will be open
- when you can get in to get your stand or stall set up
- how much time you have to get out after the show is over
- parking arrangements for your car or van
- public liability insurance
- security arrangements, if appropriate
- the exact size of your space or stand (you will need this information so that you can design your exhibit)
- power points available for lighting
- the position of your space or stand; choose a prominent space if you can, although it may be more expensive
- what the organizers need in the way of publicity material and the deadline for this
- exact venue, times and charging details for your flyers.

▶ Planning your exhibit

The first time you exhibit, planning and design will take quite a long time, so needs to be scheduled in to your work programme. Set aside the day before the show for gathering all your materials together and the day after the show for packing them away and following up any contacts you have made. This is in addition to the time taken actually designing the exhibit.

When visiting the show before the one in which you are going to exhibit, look around to see what type of customer it attracts, and how busy it is. Look, too, at exhibits similar to your own and analyse what attracts you, how easy it is to see exactly what is on offer, how easy it is to obtain information about the products exhibited, what the price range is and how the display is set up. You will probably find you are attracted by movement, perhaps a video display on a laptop, or better still a craftsperson actually at work; people will spend a long time watching a potter or a woodcarver.

Suppose you sell jewellery, where it is difficult to incorporate movement into the design. This is where good display technique comes in. Good jewellery looks good displayed on dark velvet, with a variety of levels: these do not have to be custom-made stands but can be boxes of various heights covered in the velvet. You will probably need stands on which to display the jewellery itself, and certainly a mirror. Prices can be displayed per piece on a small tag, according to a catalogue or brochure or in groups of jewellery. It is a good idea for customers to see you wearing the jewellery you sell, so you will need to wear clothing which shows off the jewellery. Wear comfortable shoes because you will be on your feet most of the day. Take spotlighting if you can – it makes the jewellery sparkle.

If you sell woodwork or leatherwork or something similar, design your space so that customers can see you working. If possible, choose something that is not too fiddly, and arrange lighting so that you can see what you are doing; consider the power points if you are using power tools. Take examples of your finished work and something on which to display it. You will also need brochures, leaflets or flyers, or a combination of these. You will certainly need price lists. It will not be possible for you to work all day, so make sure you have somewhere safe to store your tools when you are not using them. Take suitable clothing; shows in the open air can be quite cold and wet.

Whatever you sell, make a full list of everything you want to take with you – absolutely everything, including a stool to sit on, flasks of coffee and so on. These are called prop (or property) lists. You will also need something to carry your exhibits in. Tough bags with handles are easier to carry than boxes, but plastic baskets with handles are useful. Wrap things carefully and store all the carrying materials out of sight while the show is on. Include a sign so that customers can see quickly who you are.

▶ Manning your space or stand

If the show or exhibition is lasting for a long time, perhaps several weeks for an art or sculpture exhibition, it may not be possible to have the stand manned at all times. If this is the case, make sure you know what the organizers arrange, and if possible have an arrangement with a neighbouring exhibitor to look after your exhibit when you cannot be there. Customers often want someone to talk to about the exhibits.

Most shows and exhibitions last for only a few days, or possibly just one evening. It is important to make sure your exhibit is manned at all times, preferably by you and someone who knows something about your work, so they can talk knowledgeably to customers. In this way you can cover for each other when you need a break.

Remember this: Be approachable

When you are manning your stand, look inviting. People are reluctant to approach someone who is sitting reading, or in deep conversation at the back of the space. Stand at the front, handing out flyers, if appropriate; your team members can take it in turns to do this.

If it is feasible, encourage team members to wear something similar, if not identical, particularly if you have T-shirts or sweaters with your company name on them. It makes the whole team look as though they are part of the business.

Manning an exhibition space is extremely tiring, so have somewhere to sit when you can. Some businesses need a 'hospitality' area where you can sit and talk details with potential customers, and maybe offer them a coffee or a drink. If so, remember to include these items in your prop list. Do not do this without thought, however, because it can become expensive. If you sell food, little tasters are always welcome, and the same goes for a small – very small – glass of drink, but that is not the same as a hospitality area.

Collect other people's business cards, and write on the back where you got them. Some exhibitors have a large bowl for collecting cards, with a small prize for the one drawn at the end of the day. Collect cards from other exhibitors as well as from visitors. All these might be useful in the future.

When an exhibition or show is over, follow up your contacts promptly, that is within 48 hours. You will hope to sell many of your wares at the show, but sometimes that is not possible and the best you can do is make initial contact and then follow up. It is up to you to do this; do not wait for them to contact you.

Remember this: Be prepared!
Never travel anywhere without your marketing material.

Making a short presentation

For some people standing up to make a presentation to a group of people comes quite easily; to others it is a really daunting prospect. If you want to promote your business at a networking meeting, it has to be done, so seize every opportunity.

PREPARATION

Whether you welcome this opportunity or whether you dread it, preparation is vital. Every audience is different and needs a slightly different approach. First consider your anticipated audience. Write down:

1 what your audience may know already

2 what you want them to know about your business

3 what you want them to do.

To go back to the second example in Chapter 1, Sam, who is opening a boutique called Affordable Fashion, might write down for a local business networking meeting:

1 'The audience already knows the High Street and what shops are there. They also know about parking and access.'

2 'I want them to know exactly what type of clothes I will be selling, where I differ from the competition (without running them down), where my new boutique is and when it is due to open.' (All the points she identified as selling points in Chapter 1.)

3 'I want them to come to my opening, so will have my flyers with me and will mention any opening offer.'

James, who is setting up a garden consultancy business, for an audience of the local gardening club, could write down:

1 'I am aware they are all enthusiastic gardeners, and they might already have met me as manager of the garden centre. I know the local conditions and the sort of plants which thrive in the locality.'

2 'I want them to know I can advise on any kind of garden makeover from design through to execution and manage any subcontractors required. I can also help with small projects for much smaller gardens. I do not do routine garden maintenance.'

3 'I want my audience to consider the time of year at which I am speaking and to think about how they might change to lower maintenance or to bringing back the grass and introducing a wild garden. I will be putting ideas into their heads. I want them to contact me for a preliminary consultative visit, without obligation. I will have my leaflets with me.'

The content of Sam's and James' presentation will naturally follow from points 2 and 3. As far as visual aids are concerned, Sam is her own visual aid in the way she dresses and she might take a belt or handbag as examples; James may have a large photograph or two to show. In five minutes neither will have time to do a PowerPoint presentation.

Both Sam and James will need to make a prop list of all the marketing materials they want to take, including their own notes.

Notes are best made on cards, colour-coded so they can be quickly read. Use highlighters to highlight the main points you want to say, with different colours for different headings. Write large enough. Number your cards in case you drop them and have to put them together again. Cards are neater than large sheets of paper. Another advantage is that, as you put one card behind the other, your audience cannot tell how far you have got. This is not so important for a short presentation, but for a long one your audience can lose interest, particularly if they can see you still have a lot of pages to turn over.

REHEARSAL

Set aside time to rehearse your presentation, in front of a mirror or a friend. It helps you to feel confident that you have got all the points you want to make in the right order. You should also practise using any visual aids you have and wearing the clothes you are going to wear. For women, it is inadvisable to wear very short skirts or very tight trousers. When you are nervous your legs sometimes tremble, and you do not want your audience to see your knees twitching. If you can, find out the background colour of the walls or drapes, so that you do not wear the same colour. A woman in a wine-coloured suit standing against wine-coloured drapes disappears into the background, as does a man in a white shirt in front of a white screen.

Experienced speakers will have done this all before, but it is still worth rehearsing for that particular audience, particularly if you have not done it for a while. Rehearsing makes sure that your presentation will fit into the allotted time, which you must establish beforehand. Too short and you look as if you have nothing exciting to say; too long and the chair of the meeting is likely to cut you short.

Try it now: Prepare your presentation

You are almost bound to be given the opportunity to make a short presentation if you join a networking group, and it is one of the best ways of marketing your business. Start your preparation now:

✻ Write down the answer to points 1, 2 and 3 above for your business.
✻ Make a list of everything you want to take with you (your prop list). Visual aids should arise naturally out of your text, not the other way around.
✻ Prepare a five-minute presentation on cards.
✻ You will now have the foundation for any presentation you are asked to make and can quickly rehearse, without having to panic if called upon at short notice. You can adjust the notes by slotting in different cards for different audiences or for longer presentations.
✻ It may seem a little previous to do this early on, but you can use all the thoughts you have gathered together for a presentation in other circumstances such as one-to-one selling (see Chapter 5).

MAKING YOUR PRESENTATION

If you are an inexperienced speaker, follow these guidelines and practise them as you rehearse. If you are experienced, check you do all these things. Many people fidget, stand awkwardly, jingle coins or jewellery, or look down at their notes all the time without realizing they are doing so. This is where a friend whose opinion you trust is very helpful. Make it a rule not to drink, or to drink very little, before you stand up to speak. Alcohol really can dull the brain and slur your speech, if only very slightly, and you need all your wits about you.

Bear this checklist in mind:

► Check the time so you know when to finish. Remember to stick to the allotted time.

► Take a deep breath to steady your nerves.

► Relax your neck muscles by shrugging your shoulders and turning your head from side to side. While your back is temporarily to the audience, relax your face muscles by 'making faces' and yawning.

► Stand tall and balanced, head up.

► Stand where you can be seen.

► Do not lean on the furniture and do not fidget.

► Hold your cards in one hand. If you put them on the table, you will talk to the table instead of your audience.I

► Embrace the group. Turn your head and body to all sides of the group.

► There is often a 'nodder' in the group, and it is very tempting to talk exclusively to someone who seems to agree with you.

► Say your name and business clearly.

► Speak slowly and clearly, making your two or three main points with a slight pause between each.

► Demonstrate as appropriate.

▶ Refer to your printed promotional material but do not hand it out. Do that before you begin or at the end, as this disruption will drastically cut into your allotted time.

▶ Finish on a positive note with a call to action.

▶ Smile and say thank you.

When you, and all other speakers, have finished, hand out your marketing material, as appropriate, and have a notebook handy to write down contacts, queries and so on. Follow these up within 48 hours. Now you can breathe a sigh of relief, have that drink you have been promising yourself, and congratulate yourself on a good presentation. Videojug.com has a 'How to' on making a short presentation.

Focus points

✱ Marketing is an important part of your business – it takes careful thought and time.

✱ Decide which marketing tools are best for you: leaflets, brochures, flyers, your website or social networking.

✱ Network, too, with local groups and at trade and craft shows and prepare a short presentation about your business.

✱ Finally – NEVER travel without your marketing materials.

Next step

Whatever your product or service, you need to be able to sell what you are offering and sell yourself. Chapter 5 gives advice on how to get under the skin of your customers or clients, how to present your product or service, how to handle objections and, above all, when to *stop* selling!

5

Selling

In this chapter you will learn:

▶ *How to prepare for a sales meeting*
▶ *How to establish and respond to your potential customer's needs*
▶ *How to describe your product's or service's features and sell its benefits*
▶ *How to respond to customers' objections*
▶ *How to know when to stop selling*
▶ *How to sell on and sell up.*

This chapter is not about retailing, where people come to you to buy. It is about selling your product or service to potential customers on *their* territory, or possibly on *neutral* territory, such as a hotel coffee lounge.

Self-assessment: What do you know about selling?

As you complete this assessment, think of yourself and your product or service. Be explicit in your answers.

1 What makes you a good salesperson?

2 How do you get under the skin of your client or customer?

3 What should you take with you to a sales meeting?

4 What is your customer's territory?

5 How would you establish your customer's needs?

6 What are the features of your product or service?

7 What are the benefits to your customers or clients of your product or service?

8 What is selling up?

9 What is selling on?

10 When should you stop selling?

Preparation and approach

PREPARATION

Each potential customer is different, and will want to buy your product or service for slightly different reasons.

Find out as much as you can about the company or client – name, history, background, image, sales potential. Study their advertisements, their stationery, their website and anything else which will give you information about them. A copy of their annual report and accounts is useful, if they are a large, registered company. You will have to fit into their image of themselves. For example, if when speaking to you or writing to you they have automatically called you by your first name, you know they will want the same approach from you. If their stationery is of top quality, and correspondence is well written and presented, it will tell you a lot about the client's or company's image of themselves. It will tell you, for example, that they or their employees invest time and money in creating a high-quality product or service. They will expect you to do the same.

Remember to take with you samples, leaflets, models, a short laptop presentation – anything to enhance what you have to say. Take your business card and your diary, for future appointments.

Remind yourself of how this particular meeting was generated, especially if you have several calls to make, and have the names of the people you are going to meet firmly in your mind. Have your client's or customer's telephone number handy in case you get stuck in traffic, or are otherwise delayed. There is nothing worse than arriving inexplicably late.

Set yourself an objective for the meeting, which might be one of several. For example, if this is your first meeting, your objective might be to set a date when you can demonstrate your product or meet the real decision maker. If it is a later meeting, your objective might be to clinch the sale. Do not expect to achieve everything in one meeting, particularly if you are after a sizeable contract, but do try to achieve the objective you have set yourself.

Remember this: Make it personal

The more you know about your client or customer, the more likely you are to be able to meet their needs.

APPROACH

For a first meeting, the way you approach your potential client or customer is very important. Unless you are meeting on neutral ground, you will be entering your customer's territory. Take care when parking your car that you have not parked in the wrong place – blocking a neighbour's access, for example, or in reserved parking spaces. Just check it is OK to park there. Put some company identity on your dashboard, so that, if someone needs to ask you to move your car for some reason, they have some idea of where to look for you.

Take note of whoever greets you: build up a friendly relationship with receptionists, secretaries and any other 'support' people. If you are visiting people's houses, ring the bell and take a step back, so you don't appear threatening. Check you are speaking to the right person and introduce yourself. Remember to greet other members of the household if you meet them – including children and pets! Remember in all cases to say thank you for any refreshments provided. These people are all part of your customer's background and team, and can often be a help to you in the future.

Try it now: Preparing your sales visit

This is a template you can use for any sales visit. It is useful to fill it in when you make an appointment, and have it by you when you make the visit. Try it out on the next visit you make, or on a visit you are likely to make.

SALES VISIT

Client's/customer's company name:

Contact name(s) and job titles:

Address:

Email:

Telephone no.:

Mobile no.:

Type of visit (e.g. introductory, follow-up, final sale):

Your objective for the meeting:

Take with you:

Any other useful information:

Take note, too, of the environment. Is the place smart, tidy, fashionable, upmarket, disorganized, scruffy or what? Make allowances for working conditions in, say, a factory or warehouse and match your approach to the environment in which you find yourself. A chaotic place of work might mean a chaotic way of doing business. This is not to say you must lower your standards in any way, but you should try to attune yourself to your customer's style.

Once you have greeted your customer with a handshake and called him or her by the appropriate name, you will probably be expected to make the opening remarks. It is useful to be able to refer to an email and/or letter you have written, or a leaflet or sample you have sent; have a spare copy handy in case yours has got mislaid by your customer. Do not, at this stage, try to go through all the good things about your product or service; it is very tempting to reel these off, but you might not be meeting the needs of that particular customer. Before trying to sell your product or service, you must establish what those needs are.

Establishing the customer's needs

You want to find out why your customer or client needs your product or service. To do this you must get your customer talking and be very clear in your mind how your product or service is going to meet those needs.

You could ask your customers to fill you in on what the requirements actually are. For example, if you are trying to land a contract to supply executive lunches in the boardroom, it would be helpful to know, before you start displaying your wares, whether this is a new idea for this company, or whether they are dissatisfied with their present caterers, what sort of catering they had in mind and whether this is likely to be a one-off job or a longer contract. This information will then guide you into the sort of service you can offer and the cost, before getting down to details of menu, time, number and so on.

James, with his garden design and planting service, is more likely to be visiting private customers, whose needs will be different. He must establish what those needs are, and ask questions about which garden (front or back), which part of the garden, has the customer anything specific in mind (for example lawn, flowers, vegetables or all three). It is better for James to visit in the daylight, so he can be taken round the garden and establish the size of the potential job. He should have a notebook with him to jot down what the client says. When James has a good idea of what his client wants, he can begin to match his service to the client's needs.

To develop the conversation along informative lines, you will need to ask questions. Broadly speaking, there are two sorts of question – open and closed.

▶ Open questions

These are questions which begin with words like 'who', 'what', 'when', 'where', 'why' and 'how'. They cannot be answered by a simple 'yes' or 'no', and force the person answering to give you at least some information. For example, 'How have you organized these lunches in the past?' might prompt the person to answer 'We haven't, this is a new idea', or 'Well, we've dropped them recently, because we weren't too happy with them.' You have gained a lot more information than if you had asked, 'Is this a new idea for you?' (a closed question), to which the reply could be either 'yes' or 'no'.

Open questions are very useful for getting customers to open up and explain fully what their needs are.

▶ Closed questions

As you have seen, these are questions which can invite a 'yes' or 'no' answer, and are less useful for drawing information out of people.

They can, however, be useful if you want a customer to come to a decision, or make a choice. 'Would you prefer hot or cold?' will prompt either a definite choice or at least lead your customer down one road or the other. 'Shall I be here at 11.00 or 11.30?' stands more chance of getting a definite answer than 'What time would you like me here?'

Continue questioning and clarifying until you are clear about what your customer or client actually wants. If it is obvious to you that what you have to offer does not in any way meet the requirements, it is better to say so than waste your time or your customer's by trying to sell something totally unsuitable or something that you cannot deliver. Do not be put off by objections (which are dealt with later in this chapter), nor by the customer's inability to see that your product or service would be of some benefit. Stop selling at this point only if you are quite sure your product or service is unacceptable.

Features, benefits and objections

FEATURES AND BENEFITS

People buy for different reasons. At this point you have discovered what your client's or customer's real needs are. Now is the time to do two things:

1 describe the **features** of your product or service

2 sell the **benefits.**

The features are facts, the benefits are good reasons why your customer should want your product or service – and it is benefits which you must sell.

To return to the executive luncheon service, listed below are some probable features and facts about the service and the allied benefits:

EXECUTIVE LUNCHEON SERVICE	
Features	Benefits
All food prepared elsewhere and brought in	Client would save staff time buying in and preparing food
Waiter/waitress service	Prestige of expert attention to client's own customers
Wide choice of menu	Variety of tastes and dietary requirements catered for
All products bought fresh (not frozen etc.)	Excellent quality of food
Large selection of wines	Flexible to meet cost requirements
All table preparation and clearing done	No staff time taken

If your questioning revealed that these lunches had previously been done in-house, then you would emphasize the benefit of saving staff time. If it were a new idea for the company, you would mention the prestige attached to outside caterers.

You would not approach a potential customer or client without a full knowledge of your product or service, and what you can deliver; the skill is to match your product to the client's requirements by selling the benefits.

OBJECTIONS

A customer or client often has genuine objections to your product or service. Do not look upon this as an insurmountable obstacle, but as an opportunity to guide the client in the right direction by overcoming those objections.

▶ Misunderstandings

Objections sometimes arise through misunderstandings or misinterpretations in both directions. If a customer says something like 'Yes, but I'm not too sure...', try to find out where the uncertainty lies by asking questions and probing into the area of doubt. It might be that the customer has misheard or misread something, or that you have not explained it clearly. It might be that you have not understood what the client meant. Keep clarifying until you do, and then clear up the misunderstanding.

For example, if the 'Executive Luncheon' client said, 'I'm not too sure about salmon mousse as a starter,' it might be that you had given the impression that salmon mousse was the only starter available or that you had not understood that the client does not like fish. In either event by asking, 'What would you prefer as a starter?' you will probably elicit enough information to clear up the point.

▶ Scepticism

Sometimes customers or clients are doubtful about the capacity of your product or service to meet their needs. If they say something like 'Yes, but I can't see how…', you must reassure them by proving that your product or service will meet their needs.

This is the time to quote definite facts or demonstrate the product. You can show relevant tables of figures, make good estimates of time and/or money saved or literally demonstrate the product there and then. This is where your good knowledge and preparation pays off.

If the 'Executive Luncheon' client said, 'I don't see how you can get the boardroom clear in a quarter of an hour,' you could quote other examples (named clients) of where you had done that, or you could take the client quickly through the timings, emphasizing the fact that everything is brought in easily packed trays.

▶ Price

One of the most common objections is the cost. You must be very sure in your own mind how low you can go in accepting a lower cost, and be flexible down to that point. You can emphasize the fact that VAT is recoverable (if it is); you should also restate the agreed benefits to the customer.

You might be able to go lower on one point (perhaps reduce the delivery charge) while sticking on another. Sometimes it is better to quote for the whole package, while emphasizing what the package contains. At others it is useful to 'unbundle' the package (cost each element separately), so the client can buy at least some of it.

Try not to let the customer buy only the least profitable parts of the package. For example, the 'Executive Luncheon' firm would be unwise to let the client provide the wine, because that is probably the most profitable part of the business. However, if such a deal were to lead to a long and good contract, the firm might decide to let it go this time and renegotiate another time.

Be prepared to negotiate on price as on other aspects of the deal, but know your limits.

Closing

The customer will eventually give an indication that he or she is ready to bring the meeting to a close. The signs might be verbal: 'Well, if you would like to let me have a copy of those figures for Monday morning...' or 'Yes, I like what you're offering, but I need to consult my colleagues.' The signs might be non-verbal – nodding; leaning forward, hands on thighs; standing up.

When you receive these closing signals STOP SELLING. More than one sale has been lost by the salesperson overemphasizing agreed benefits or, worse still, introducing benefits not mentioned before, which only confuses the customer. It is not easy to stop yourself from telling the customer *all* the benefits of your product or service, but once the closing signals have been given, you must stop selling.

Summarize what has been agreed between you:

▶ If a new meeting is to be arranged, try to arrange it then and there – get your diary out and suggest dates and times.

▶ If a senior executive asks you to make an appointment with his or her PA, make it with the PA and do not try and force the executive to make the appointment.

▶ If you are to provide further information, establish exactly when and where it is to be delivered.

▶ If your customer is to let you have further information, try to get a definite commitment on what it is and the anticipated timing.

▶ If the person to whom you are speaking is not the decision maker, try to make sure that your product or service gets

presented to the decision maker. Try to get a name, and offer
to write or meet to demonstrate the product – anything to
take the matter a step further

If you are able to clinch the sale at that meeting, make sure
that *all* costs, delivery dates and so on are agreed, and get a
signature if possible. Immediately after the meeting, write and
confirm the terms of the agreement, set out very clearly what
you are supplying, what the costs are and what the terms of
payment are. If you think it more than likely that this meeting
will be the one where you finally make the sale, you can have all
this paperwork ready with you, but do not produce it too early
in the proceedings.

At the close of the meeting, each party should be clear about
what is to happen next on both sides. This applies to a service
rendered in someone's home just as much as it does to a product
sold to a large company. Shake hands to conclude the meeting.

> **Remember this:** Courtesy costs nothing
>
> As you leave, don't forget to say goodbye to support staff or other
> members of the household, and thank them for anything they have done
> for you.

Finally, when you get back to your own place of work, do
everything that you have promised to do, and do it promptly.

When you can, analyse how well the meeting went. These are
some guidelines to help with your analysis:

▶ Did you achieve your objective(s)?

▶ If not, why not?

▶ Did you push the product or service without establishing the
customer's or client's needs?

▶ Did you sell the appropriate benefits?

▶ Could you meet the objections?

▶ Did you recognize the closing signals?

▶ Did you oversell?

▶ Was your product or service just not right for that customer or client at that time?

▶ If so, can you go back another time?

Selling up and selling on

When you have established the main sale, you might be able to sell up or sell on.

▶ **Selling up** is persuading your client that the more expensive option would best meet their needs. For example, James might persuade his gardening customer that oak posts for the fence would be better than softwood.

▶ **Selling on** is selling something extra. James suggesting he could do the planting as well as buying the plants. His client may or may not want the oak posts and the extra work done; the secret is to put these ideas in your customer's or client's mind, but not to be too pushy, or you may lose the sale altogether. Selling on is selling extras, not things which come as standard.

Remember this: Note the difference

Selling up is selling something 'instead of' and selling on is selling something 'as well as'.

The 'Executive Luncheon' business could suggest that English wines are a nice touch, because their reputation has grown, and their carbon footprint is smaller, although they are a little more expensive; here the salesperson would be selling the benefits of English wines and selling up to a slightly more expensive, more profitable level. The salesperson could also suggest something extra, for example their new (a hook word) menu-printing service.

There are many ways in which you can sell up and sell on, so this next exercise asks you to think along these lines.

Against the various types of business, fill in the gaps by thinking of the sorts of things they might sell up or sell on, then do the same for your own business. You might like to pick a business closest to your own. We have included a couple of ideas against each business to start you off. Sometimes either the one or the other is impossible.

Business	Selling up (Instead of)	Selling on (As well as)
Home hairdresser:	Best conditioner	Sell a special shampoo
Accountant:		Book-keeping service
Management consultant:	Team activity day instead of room-based day	
Small machine tool manufacturer:	Greater precision for certain products	Additional tools for customer's new machines
Artist/craftsperson:	Better-quality materials	Framing service
Central heating engineer:	Programmable installation	Maintenance agreement
Painter and decorator:	Top-quality paint for exterior	
Curtain/blind supplier:	Heavier fabric to hang better	Curtain pole installation
Manicurist:	Gel instead of varnish	Toes as well as fingers
Window cleaner:		Inside as well as out
Your own business:		

Next step

The next step, or perhaps the first step, is e-commerce, selling online. Chapter 6 explores how to get started, how best to display your wares and how to organize your ordering, payment and despatch. It also covers copyright and marketing, but starts, as does any other business, with market research.

E-commerce

In this chapter you will learn how to:

▶ *Consider whether e-commerce is a viable prospect for your business and to what extent*

▶ *How to develop and run an effective e-commerce website*

▶ *Deal with tricky issues such as postage and packing and returns*

▶ *Sell through eBay, including opening an eBay shop, and consider an alternative such as Etsy.*

Perhaps you've decided to sell your products online from the start, or after you've been running your business for a while. You'll no longer be selling face to face, and won't know who your customers are.

Self-assessment: What do you know about e-commerce?

This assessment is designed to start you thinking about the various aspects of selling online. The chapter will help you get started in an efficient way, and includes a detailed case study of one small company, run by one person who decided to expand her existing business and sell worldwide. It's called 'Caroline's story'.

1 What market research should you do to sell online?
2 Where could you get help and advice?
3 Who will design your website?
4 Who will maintain your website?
5 What is eBay and how will it help you?
6 What is Etsy, and would it be right for you?
7 Who will take your photographs?
8 What is PayPal?
9 What is your returns policy likely to be?
10 How will you despatch your products?
11 What is the best way to market your online business?

Market research

Try it now: Look at your competitors' websites

One of the first things to do is to look at the websites which sell products similar to your own. As you do this, answer the following questions:

✽ What sort of things do they sell?
✽ How easy is it to find your way around the site?
✽ What do you like about it?
✽ What don't you like?

By the time you have visited three or four of these sites, you will have a good idea of what you want for your own business.

Getting started

YOUR WEBSITE NAME

Once you have decided to go ahead with selling online, you need to register your website name. If you are already in business you will be able to use the same name, or something very similar, for your website name. If you are selling online from the start, you can choose your own company name, making sure you incorporate in the name something which indicates the nature of your business if possible. 'Carousel Creations', for example, could be about almost anything, but 'Carousel Cottage Crafts' indicates much more clearly what the products are likely to be.

REGISTERING YOUR WEBSITE NAME

Next, check whether your company name is available on '.co. uk' and on '.com'. The first caters for the UK market, and the second reaches the market worldwide, especially the USA. When you try to register your own name through an ISP (Internet Service Provider) you will very quickly find out whether the name you have chosen is available or not. You might have to tweak it slightly to register it. Once your name is registered, it will become accessible to anybody with an Internet connection. You would need to make a decision as to whether to register your name as '.co.uk' or '.com', or both, or that of another domain such as .net.

If you register both '.co.uk' and '.com', it means that nobody can register their company on '.co.uk' using your name, which they could do if you registered for '.com' only. If you intend selling internationally (incurring the complication of despatching products to overseas addresses), then register as '.com'. If, however, your business is focused on the UK, go for '.co.uk' only, to get the highest possible ratings in local search engines such as Google.co.uk. And do not forget '.eu' if your company's focus is primarily European.

DESIGNING YOUR WEBSITE

If you are computer literate you might be able to design your own website using a free e-commerce package such as Zen Cart, which is a good place to start if e-commerce is likely to be a major, or only, part of your new business.

A hosted service can be a good option for new businesses. In this case a company (often an ISP) provides a complete online service, including buying domain names, setting up and managing an online shop and dealing with payments, while the small business simply enters its products – though the work involved in 'simply entering products' should not be underestimated. The drawback of this approach is that the range of e-commerce options is often quite narrow and the shop owner has no control over expanding them.

If your e-commerce is likely to be an add-on to a real-world business, with just a few products, it is worth starting with a hosted service to see how it goes; this way you can achieve credibility and a few sales for minimal effort and cost. If the e-commerce really takes off, you can upgrade to a more comprehensive website, designed especially for your business.

Many people cannot at first go beyond word processing, spreadsheets and photograph manipulation, so for them using a good website designer is probably the answer. Go for a small company or a sole trader who is maybe starting out themselves. You can usually get to know who they are through networking meetings.

You may well wish to have your own, exclusive design, which is the next step to take. You will need a series of website pages, which usually include:

- ▶ a home page (introducing your products to the world)

- ▶ different pages for various categories of product

- ▶ a page for ordering and paying

- ▶ a 'Contact Us' page, with all your contact details

- ▶ a page 'About Us'.

Your home page will include your name and logo and take account of your company colours, if you have any. Include a well-written paragraph or two that describes your products and what makes them different. Search engines love this, and, happily, your USP (unique selling point) is often a hook to turn a potential customer's passing interest into an actual sale. Make sure there is a prominent phone number on the site as well as on the 'Contact Us' page. People do like to ring and discuss your products.

An 'About Us' page is absolutely key for smaller businesses, especially start-ups, which do not have the recognition that goes with a high-street presence and lots of advertising spend. Pictures of a shop, a warehouse, a workshop, the staff, even the company cat, all help to make the business behind an Internet site more real to online customers and provide assurance and comfort.

You will also need a page or section for shipping information, together with terms of business (no goods sent until payment is received, for example), a returns policy, possible size charts, in metric and imperial where applicable, and wholesale and retail prices. A returns policy will usually state that if goods are returned within a certain time in good order, a refund will be paid; refunds are simpler than credit. Wholesalers often themselves buy on a 'sale or return' basis, which means you might get your products returned at a much later date, which could be awkward, particularly if the products are seasonal.

Remember this: Employ a copywriter

If you find it difficult to describe your product briefly, accurately and with 'sparkle', it might be money well spent to employ a professional copywriter.

You should be aware that pages describing your products take a long time to compile and can quickly proliferate into hundreds of pages. This will most likely prove to be the single biggest and most underestimated task, and is really separate from writing the general text for the site. It is also the task that can really differentiate stores as far as search engines are concerned and therefore drive traffic to a site. There is one short cut you might be able to use if you sell products made by someone else. The manufacturer or importer will often provide product descriptions that retailers are allowed to use. These descriptions are often written with the trade in mind, but you could use them as a basis and rewrite them with a little more sparkle. Whichever route you choose to follow, you need to allow plenty of time for this task, and to match descriptions to your photographs.

Do get someone to check the text for spelling and grammar and punctuation. You are not writing an English essay, but your product description does need to be clear and correctly spelled. If it is right, no one will notice it, but mistakes will put some people off. Even if your English language skills are good, get someone else to proofread your pages for you; it is difficult to proofread your own work, and proofreading on screen is more problematic than proofreading on hard copy.

Case study: Caroline's story so far

Caroline is a seamstress and embroiderer, and made and sold all sorts of country-craft items such as scented pillows and bags decorated with appliqué and embroidery, trading as Carousel Creations. The business was moderately successful locally and kept Caroline reasonably busy, but she felt she could expand into selling online and become an e-commerce business. She had basic computer skills, coping with word processing, spreadsheets and photographs, but anything beyond that she viewed with trepidation. Selling online sounded scary. She was fortunate in having a background as a financial adviser, so book-keeping and accounting were no problem; she also had a husband well versed in photography, and was no mean photographer herself.

One of her first steps was to get in touch with the Department for Work and Pensions, which offered six-month support. She was appointed a business adviser, whom she met on a fortnightly basis. This adviser helped her prepare and refine her business plan and set her targets for the next two weeks. Caroline works best when she has a deadline to meet, so this system worked well for her.

She was lucky to have a friend who was starting up his own small business as a website designer, and asked Caroline to be his first customer. Together they did a lot of research on the Net. Which similar businesses were there already? What website names were available? What did they like about other people's websites and what didn't they like? How were these websites and their products marketed and advertised? They found eBay a very good selling medium, because as well as normal listings for private transactions, eBay also allows you to sell on a commercial basis. You can also open up an eBay shop, a sort of showcase for your products. They stored this information up for future reference.

Now for a website name. Carousel Creations didn't actually say what the company sold, and anyway the name wasn't available on '.co.uk' and '.com'. So they changed the trading name to Carousel Cottage Crafts, which they could register for both '.co.uk' for UK business and '.com' for business worldwide. Her friend the website designer saw to all this for her and together they designed the structure of her website. This included her home page, with an introduction to the company and its products, several pages of product photographs and descriptions, a 'policy' page, an ordering and payment facility and a 'Contact Us' page. Caroline put her business email address on this page towards the back of the website so that if people wanted it they could find it. Incidentally, she had established a business email address and a private email address. It's always better to keep your business life and your private life separate, if you can. An email address can attract a lot of spam, but Caroline didn't find this too much of a problem, as her Internet Service Provider was quite good at filtering out the spam.

Caroline felt she could perfectly well write the descriptions of her products, with sizes where appropriate, and a catalogue number herself. Of course, she emphasized her unique selling points – all hand-made in England – especially for the American market. She also had a digital camera good enough to take high-quality photographs and was able to refine these using Photoshop. She airbrushed out all the background, and made sure they were of a consistent size (400 pixels square) on the same background as her web pages – a sort of country-looking weave, of course. This task, compiling her 118 product pages, took ages, much longer than she had anticipated.

They decided to use a website e-commerce package called Zen Cart, a free platform for her website design. The site used photographs of her embroidery designs, with a thatched cottage logo, using a patchwork border plus sewing accessories, thread, scissors, pincushion and so on. All very country crafts.

Again she was lucky. Fairly soon after she started trading, she obtained an order from someone about to open a shop selling the types of things she makes – a wholesale order. That was on a sale and no return basis. She found later that many wholesale orders are on a sale or return basis, so it was possible for goods to be returned quite a long time later, not having been sold and therefore not paid for. Christmas bags returned in March? Not very profitable. Caroline doesn't enjoy cold-calling on shops to sell her wares, so she decided to concentrate on the retail side, selling to individual customers.

Try it now: Put together your website team

This is the time to make decisions on who will design your website, who will take the photographs of your products and who will write your product descriptions. The people who do these tasks have to work closely together.

PHOTOGRAPHS

Websites cry out for good photographs and/or moving images. Movement attracts the eye, but your website designer will advise you on this. Again, it depends on your experience with your own digital camera and your expertise in manipulating your photographs on your computer. You can certainly learn these skills, given time. A good digital camera, with flash, should be enough not to need extra lighting, although you will want to be sure you have a reasonable light source to pick up highlights on your product. Manipulate, or refine, each photograph so that there is no background (you can airbrush this out), and it is mounted on a backing the same as the website page. Photographs should also be of a consistent size of, say, 400 pixels square. If you are reasonably adept, you probably do not need any more software for creating your pages than Word or another word-processing program for the text and Photoshop (or similar) for the photographs.

COSTING YOUR PRODUCT

Chapter 2 looked at costing your product, so you can work out the basic price of each item. To that you might need to add postage and packing, which you can do on a sliding scale, depending on the amount your buyer spends. However, it is probably easier to say that postage and packing is free for UK addresses (eBay has special offers if you do this), and that people ordering from overseas should contact you first to find out the cost they will need to add to their order. Shipping costs are often on a sliding scale, perhaps free over £50. Use second-class post for the UK and airmail for all other destinations. Make friends with your local post office; you will be bringing them plenty of business. If you are VAT-registered and selling in the UK, you will need to add VAT to the cost, after all other calculations have been made. Make it clear whether the UK price is inclusive or exclusive of VAT.

COPYRIGHT

When you design and sell your products, you must take care not to infringe other people's copyright or intellectual rights. As a rule of thumb, do not copy other people's designs or ideas.

As always, it depends on what type of product you are selling, but, whatever it is, it will have been designed and made by someone, usually you, yourself. If you carry out the whole creation from start to finish, there is no problem, but if you create a product using a design you have seen somewhere else, you might fall foul of the copyright laws. Perhaps you sell pictures; if the picture is entirely your own, perhaps copied from a photograph you have taken yourself, fine, but if it is taken from a photograph in a magazine or some source other than yourself, you do not know with whom the copyright lies, and you might be breaching someone else's copyright. If you are ever accused of doing this, do three things:

1 ask for details of the alleged breach

2 make no comment

3 contact your lawyer.

It is almost impossible to protect copyright on the Internet, including your own.

Open an eBay shop

If you are not used to eBay, the first thing to do is to buy an item or two for your personal use and then sell something that you already own but no longer need. This will give you a good idea of how the whole concept of eBay works.

To open an eBay shop you must, in addition to registering as a business with eBay (you cannot buy or make items for resale as a business while pretending to be a private seller), create a seller's account, which verifies your identity and sets up your arrangements with eBay for paying your seller's fees. You must also have earned a feedback score of 10 or more, so you will need to have successfully sold a few items on eBay before you can proceed to opening a shop.

For people just starting out, the Basic Shop is the best bet. It gives an affordable online presence. It is possible to start on a low level and upgrade as your business grows.

YOUR EBAY SELLING CHECKLIST

▶ **Look at your product.** Make notes on it – if it's new, you need to say so as this is what many buyers look for and they will ignore anything that does not specifically state that it is new. Make sure you note the brand, the size and any details that buyers will want to know. Investing time now to look at your products from the buyer's point of view and taking into account just how your competitors describe and sell similar products will pay dividends in the form of higher sales later.

▶ **Take good pictures.** A plain background will show off your products to best effect and, if you're selling a wide variety of products, don't forget to download them on to your computer and label them clearly according to what each one depicts.

▶ **Weigh each item you're listing so that you can decide how you will send it and how much it will cost you.** The eBay system allows you to add a delivery and package charge to each item listed. Take care that you don't charge too much and make yourself uncompetitive (and excessive postage and packing charges are not permitted by eBay), or too little so that you will be out of pocket. There is a comprehensive guide to postage and packing on the eBay website and the Royal Mail and Parcelforce Worldwide websites (www. royalmail.com and www.parcelforce.com) have all the information you will need to work out how to pack and send your products. You can even use their online calculators and print postage labels (paying via PayPal).

▶ **Choose a good title.** It should clearly describe your product and contain all the keywords that a buyer may search for when looking for this item. This could include age, condition, brand, size, colour, model, specifications and so on. You have 55 characters available for this, so try to use them all but don't waste any. Using adjectives such as pretty, nice or valuable is usually a waste of your valuable characters as buyers do not use these words in their searches. This is a vital part of the process, so don't rush it. Get the title right and more people will view your product.

- **Follow all the listing instructions carefully and look out for hints and tips along the way.** eBay are particularly good at directing and helping new sellers so take advantage of what's available. Another resource that you will find useful is the Community section of the website. Here you can get advice from other eBay members, join discussion groups on any eBay-related topic and find out about potential customers or suppliers in the Feedback Forum. You can list in three formats – Auction-style, Fixed Price and Shop Inventory. The Auction-style is probably what eBay is best known for, where items are listed with a starting price, buyers bid on the item and items go to the highest bidder. With the Fixed Price option the seller sets a 'Buy it Now' price. Items listed in this way attract buyers who want their items quickly and who want to know exactly what they must pay for it. The Shop Inventory format is only available to sellers who have opened a shop and there is a different listings fee structure in place. Items can be listed indefinitely using this format and no auction takes place.

- **Send an invoice** – this is automated on eBay.

- **Despatch the goods when you've received payment** – note that, if you accept payments via PayPal or can accept credit cards, you will not need to wait for cheques to clear and this will result in a better service for your customers – and you'll get your money quicker, too. Make sure you've done your preparation for despatch so that you have appropriate packaging available and can send out orders quickly.

- **Give feedback.** This is part of your customer service. If someone has sent prompt payment, then say so. If you give positive feedback where it's due, then you are far more likely to receive positive feedback for your business and this is how you will build your reputation as a seller on eBay.

Ordering, payment, despatch and returns

Your customers will want to be able to order and pay as simply as possible, so make sure your products are fully described, with a catalogue number and facilities for ordering different sizes or colours, if applicable. They will then select their items and send them to their 'shopping basket'. Even here, think of your image and decide whether you want your shopping icon to look like a supermarket trolley, or indeed any other type of shopping container, perhaps even a carrier bag. Maintain your image throughout your website.

The safest and quickest way of making and receiving payment is through an 'agency' like PayPal, which is a secure method of conducting financial transactions and retains the confidentiality of your customer's bank account or credit card. Good e-commerce programs such as Zen Cart provide access to many payment processors, but for a small business starting up, PayPal is a quick and easy solution. Payment is cleared straight away, so you can quickly get the goods packed up and sent off. It also sends an automatic acknowledgement to the customer.

For your own books you will need to raise an invoice for each order, and place a copy, as a despatch note, in with the goods when you send them. It is possible to pay by e-cheque, but these take up to 15 days to clear. Do not send the goods until the cheque has arrived and is cleared, but be sure to make this clear to your customer. Take cash from personal transactions only (you still have to raise an invoice).

Your website should include a returns policy. Will you accept returns if the product is unsuitable or damaged? How long will you allow customers to return your goods? Will you refund the money, or give your customers credit on their next purchase?

It is probably better to refund the money, as your customer may not order any more of your products. Look at other people's websites to see what their returns policy is.

Marketing your website

Choosing a good name for your website, plus a strapline (a short description of what you sell) which contains words which are easily picked up by a search engine, is the first step towards marketing your product worldwide. You can also enter your products on eBay listings, but are not allowed to refer to your website trading name, or accept cash payments (in case you might be money laundering). However, if you sell through eBay, send, with the goods, a receipt which refers to your website. You can also set up a shop window on eBay, which is worth looking into.

Do not neglect your personal contacts, family, friends, business acquaintances through networking, and so on. Chapter 4 talks about flyers, leaflets and brochures, which are all marketing tools you can use to advertise your website, not forgetting your business cards. If your products are fairly standard, it is worth thinking about a hard-copy brochure, or even a catalogue; however, if your products are customized or are likely to change frequently, a brochure is less useful. If your products are seasonal – gifts for Christmas, say – do put a deadline of early December as the last ordering date or you may find yourself still making up orders on Christmas Eve – not good for the business image, or your nerves!

Case study: Caroline's story continued and continuing

The cost of each item was already pretty firmly established because Caroline had been selling in the 'normal' way, and her prices seemed to compare favourably with other, similar items. At first, she charged for postage and packing on a sliding scale, but found this too complicated, and ended up selling with free postage and packing for the UK, sending her products through her local post office, which now knew her very well – good business for them, too. Overseas buyers have to contact Caroline to find out what the airmail postage and packing costs will be and add it to their order.

As well as this shipping policy, Caroline had written into the website a returns policy; if goods were returned within a certain time limit and in good order, she would refund the payment. Actually, she found very few items returned. She had also set down her terms of business: if her customers paid through PayPal (more of this shortly) she could send off the items almost straight away, unless they were customized with names or special designs. If customers paid by e-cheque it took an unbelievable 15 days or so for the cheque to clear. Her policy was not to despatch goods until payment had been received one way or another.

Carousel Cottage Crafts' ordering and payment was a crucial part of her website: it had to be simple and, if possible, foolproof. The online order form had to allow for all the variations in her products, including size, colour and customization, and also had to include the catalogue number, quantity, the cost per item, the total cost and postage and packing where relevant. Caroline was not VAT-registered, so did not have to add VAT for her UK customers.

Once the items had been selected, her customers would send their chosen items to their shopping basket – except that the icon supplied looked like a supermarket trolley – so her website designer changed it to look like a wicker shopping basket. Zen Cart then gave her customer the link to pay through PayPal.

Every transaction had to be invoiced for her own records, but Caroline made sure to put a copy of the invoice, as a despatch note, in with the consignment. No problem for her, she was used to dealing with that sort of thing. One thing she did have to check, however, was copyright. Perhaps the design of a bag was entirely her own, but was the embroidery a copy of a design she'd discovered elsewhere? If so, she couldn't use it without express permission, and perhaps payment. So she had to make sure that the embroidery was sufficiently different not to breach someone else's copyright, and not to infringe their intellectual property rights on their design, either.

What about marketing? How would her potential customers know she existed? Her website name would easily be reached through a search engine, particularly as she had written a couple of enticing paragraphs on her home page, describing her products and her unique selling points. Caroline found her eBay listings a very good marketing tool, but of course they have to be paid for, so she's exploring opening up an eBay 'shop', which might be a more economical way of marketing through eBay.

One of her products, Christmas bags with customized names, is very seasonal. The first Christmas she made the mistake of not putting an ordering deadline of, say, 7 December on her website, and found she had an order for half a dozen customized Christmas bags about a week before Christmas. Panic stations, but she got them done and learned her lesson. She didn't neglect her normal marketing outlets, either, making sure her flyers, her postcard in the post office window, her business cards and her networking contacts all knew about her exciting new e-commerce business.

Caroline knew she needed to account for all her e-commerce business expenditure in her books and realized that, had she not had this knowledge herself, she would have needed advice from her accountant, or HM Revenue & Customs or the Department of Work and Pensions. There's plenty of help out there if you ask for it.

Caroline now runs a successful, but not overwhelming, e-commerce business. It's taken about a year to iron out all the wrinkles and get herself firmly established, but she's now happy to know that her products have been sent out to Australasia, Europe and North America. Caroline is a truly international businesswoman, and she has kindly agreed to her story being told in this book.

Once your business is up and running you can include testimonials, related to your specific products, on a separate page or on your home page. Do not be tempted to make them up!

Case study: Eva's Etsy Story

There are alternatives to eBay. Eva chose Etsy for her online selling business. Why? Eva lives and works in Portugal, where there are no large indigenous well-known international selling websites; Etsy was a natural choice for a local craftsperson to engage with an international market. Etsy is very big in the USA and is spreading rapidly into the UK and the EU. Etsy started out as a platform for selling craftware, but is now becoming more general.

Eva started her business painting designer t-shirts for children. The designs were all her own, so she had no copyright problems but competition in this field is fierce, especially because of cheaper t-shirt printers. However, after some time, Eva discovered a less competitive niche market whose needs her talents could meet, which was hand-making children's felt masks for parties and similar gatherings, so this became the main focus of her now successful business, for which Etsy suits her very well.

Her business (BHB Kidstyle) is seasonal, like Caroline's, particularly before Halloween and Christmas. She has to manage customers' expectations and make them aware of shipping times, which are out of her own control. This sometimes means that, although every order is important, she has to reject an order and refund the money because the product would not reach the customer in time. This results in a loss of income but maintains her reputation for reliability.

It took Eva two years to get her business off the ground but, like Caroline, she now sells worldwide – using English, not Portuguese or Hungarian, throughout.

If eBay doesn't suit you, consider trying another online selling outlet such as Etsy. It's worth shopping around.

Try it now: E-commerce checklist

Finally, complete this checklist to make sure you have taken all the appropriate steps to get your e-commerce business profitably up and running. Some might not apply to your business.

Have you:

1 checked out your competitors? ☐
2 chosen your website name and logo? ☐
3 registered your website name? ☐
4 decided who is to design your website? ☐
5 decided who is to maintain your website? ☐
6 written the text for your website? ☐
7 compiled your product description pages? ☐
8 taken and refined your photographs? ☐
9 written down your terms of business? ☐
10 written a returns policy? ☐
11 created a size chart? ☐
12 written your wholesale and retail policies? ☐
13 got someone else to proofread your website pages? ☐
14 decided on your postage and packing policy? ☐
15 created your Ordering web page? ☐
16 decided on your payments methods? ☐
17 checked for any copyright problems? ☐
18 marketed your products online? ☐
19 marketed your e-commerce locally? ☐
20 collected testimonials? ☐
21 set up a system for invoicing, recording expenditures ☐
     in your books, etc.?

This all sounds rather complicated, but it need not be if you take it step by step. It is certainly an interesting and profitable way of selling, worldwide.

Focus points

* Selling online can be a very profitable and exciting way of doing business.
* However, it doesn't happen overnight. Allow up to two years, if you are starting from scratch, to design your website, photograph and describe your products (this takes ages), set up your ordering and payment methods and begin to build your customer base.
* Take it step by step, and good luck!

Next step

Whatever your method of trading and the way you sell your products or services, you will have to 'do the paperwork'. Chapter 7 tackles the mundane but necessary business aspects of doing the books: banking, insurance, personal finance and allowable business expenses. To make a profit you must have a good system for dealing with your business and personal finances.

Business and personal finance

In this chapter you will learn:

▶ *How to find a good accountant – crucial if you are going to build a successful small business*

▶ *How to keep records of your income and expenditure, either manually or electronically*

▶ *How to run a business bank account*

▶ *How to deal with insurance and personal finance*

▶ *How to deal with VAT and to submit your VAT returns*

▶ *How to distinguish between allowable and non-allowable expenses.*

You are in business to make a profit, so finance, both business and personal, is an integral part of your working life. You need to be able to do the regular book-keeping and banking, take out the necessary insurance, do the end-of-year accounts, deal with HM Revenue & Customs and still have enough to live on. In all these instances your accountant will become one of the most important people in your life.

Self-assessment: What do you know about business finance?

1 When choosing your accountant, what do ACA, FCA, ACCA and FCCA stand for? Your accountant should be one of these.

2 What does CPD stand for?

3 When do self-assessment tax returns have to be with HMRC?

4 What does HMRC stand for?

5 What is petty cash?

6 You must register for VAT when your turnover reaches what figure?

7 Why should you have a business bank account?

8 What insurances will you need?

9 Will you be liable for NI (National Insurance) contributions?

10 You will be able to deduct allowable business expenses from your profits. These are complicated and numerous. For example: Is a gift to a client or customer tax deductible?

Choosing your accountant

If you do not already have an accountant, choose one early on in your new business venture. It is a venture, or an adventure, and sound advice from someone who knows what they are talking about is essential. How do you find a good accountant?

You are seeking someone who specializes in small businesses, and may even specialize in your particular line of business. You will need someone who will tell you straight out when your business is faltering, or indeed when it is doing well. An accountant can see the bigger picture, bringing his or her expertise to bear on your business, and should be a sound adviser, someone you can talk to openly without fear of being ridiculed or bamboozled by jargon. Never hide things from your accountant, who needs to know all your financial circumstances before giving advice. If you are not business or financially minded yourself, you need someone who can explain to you, in words of one syllable if necessary, exactly what it all means. After all, your accountant can only advise: it is up to you to make decisions and instruct your accountant accordingly.

You need an accountant who is suitably qualified. In the UK the word 'accountant' is not protected by law, so make sure your accountant is either a Chartered Accountant (ACA or FCA after his or her name) or a Chartered Certified Accountant (ACCA or FCCA). They all have to earn their CPD (Continued Professional Development) points to keep themselves up to date.

Personal recommendation by someone whose opinion you trust is a good start, but you would be wise to enquire into two or three accountants before choosing the right person for you. Meet them, and judge whether they are the kind of person you can work with. Establish what their annual charges are likely to be and exactly what they will be charging for, and get this in writing if you can.

Small firms of accountants, or sole proprietors, are often the best people for very small businesses, because that is what they do themselves – they run their own small business and understand how you work. It is better to avoid the large firms, who tend to be expensive, although they might have a small business specialist on the team. Make sure you meet the person who will actually be looking after your accounts, not a senior partner who will then pass you on to someone junior you have not met.

After personal recommendation comes impartial advice, perhaps from local business groups or your Chamber of Commerce, or the Institute of Chartered Accountants in England and Wales (see *Yellow Pages*). Accountants are allowed to advertise, but if you know nothing about them it is difficult to choose the best person for your business, although you may find firms who specialize in your line of business or are experienced in the book-keeping software you use. The large, colourful adverts are usually placed by the larger firms. One thing in favour of larger firms is that they do specialize in various aspects of accounting, such as employment or investment and portfolio building, or, indeed, small business accounting.

In the end only you and your business partner can decide which accountant to choose. Make sure that all partners or directors meet the person concerned and can get on with him or her. You do not have to be close friends, but you will be working closely together, perhaps for many years.

WHAT YOUR ACCOUNTANT CAN DO FOR YOU

First, your accountant can, and usually does, put together your end-of-year accounts to present to whichever authorities require to see them. This includes Companies House, for a limited company, the Charity Commissioners, for a registered charity, and of course HM Revenue & Customs (HMRC) to assess what your business needs to pay in the way of corporation tax.

Your accountant will also send in your tax returns to HMRC for your personal income, which includes such things as returns on investments and savings and rent on properties you own. Your personal income tax is separate from your business tax, but if, for example, you are a partner in a partnership, your tax liability for your business is sent in at the same time as your personal tax return.

Self-assessment tax returns can be done by your accountant and sent in by the end of September. If you want HMRC to assess what you owe, your tax return must be sent in by the end of December (these are the rules current in 2015). If you fail to send in your tax returns on time, you may be liable to a fine.

So, your accountant will:

▶ put together your end-of-year accounts (from the date when your business started, or the end of the government's financial year on 4 April)

▶ go through these accounts with you and ask you to sign them as a true record

- submit them to the appropriate authorities

- calculate the tax you owe HMRC and submit your self-assessment tax returns.

Your accountant can do much more than this, however. He or she can, and will at a cost, do your book-keeping for you, send in your VAT returns if you are VAT-registered, act as financial adviser to you and your business and train you in the best and clearest way to do your own book-keeping if you do that yourself. Specialist accountants can also advise on the complexities of farm payments, if you are a farmer, for example, or the employment of migratory workers if you are a registered gangmaster. He or she can also be present at interviews or meetings with your bank, HMRC or any other 'authority' with whom you come into contact. Wages and salaries can also be done by your accountant or your book-keeper. Of course, you will be charged for each aspect of the service, which is why it is important for you to decide what you can do yourself, and where it is better to employ the professional. However much or little you ask your accountant to do, there are many things you can do to help.

WHAT YOU CAN DO FOR YOUR ACCOUNTANT

Your accountant, even if the annual accounts is the limit of his or her involvement, will need to establish an audit trail, so that your accounts can be 'signed off'. Therefore there are several things you can do to help:

- Follow the book-keeping methods, electronic or manual, agreed between you.

- Keep all receipts for everything, including petty cash.

- Be meticulous in recording every item of income and expenditure.

- Tell the truth about all your financial dealings. If you are found to have been economical with the truth, your accountant will not have a leg to stand on when dealing with HMRC, for example. Be aware that an apparently innocent question, unless honestly answered, could lead your accountant down the wrong path.

- ▶ Let your accountant have your end-of-year accounts as soon as possible so that self-assessment can be calculated in time not to incur penalties.

- ▶ Do your books regularly and keep them up-to-date.

- ▶ Ask your accountant's advice before embarking on a big expansion programme or any adjustment to your business you want to set up.

- ▶ Let your accountant know of any change in personnel in your business, or any change in your personal status – marriage, for example.

You can see how you and your accountant need to work closely together.

Try it now: Choose your accountant

This form should help you decide on who you want to be your accountant and how much you want him or her to do on your behalf.

What do you want your accountant to do?

End-of-year (annual) accounts	☐
Business tax returns	☐
Personal tax returns	☐
Book-keeping	☐
Wages and salaries	☐
VAT returns	☐
Advice and guidance	☐
Personal finance advice (e.g. investment and inheritance tax)	☐

Who is, or will be, your accountant?

Name (with qualifications):

Address (someone near you is a good idea):

Telephone number:

Email address:

Doing the books

As you have seen, accountancy and book-keeping are two different things. Whether you decide to do the book-keeping yourself, or whether you employ a professional book-keeper (or accountant), the key to successful, and not excessively time-consuming, book-keeping is to have a workable system, to keep to it, and so keep on top of the workload. This section describes doing the books manually, followed by advice on book-keeping on your desktop or laptop.

It is highly likely that you will do your book-keeping electronically. The principles outlined in this section will still apply, but the software will do the calculations for you.

RECORDING RECEIPTS AND PAYMENTS

Broadly speaking, the books of a business are divided into two sections, one to record moneys coming in and the other to record moneys going out. An average small business does not need to have a complicated system of book-keeping, but it does need to show clearly the incomings and outgoings of the business, and dates when the transactions took place. A very simple system could look like Figure 7.1.

However, it would not be very practical, because you will want to analyse receipts and payments (particularly payments) under different headings at the time of recording the details in the books: this can be done with very little effort or trouble. It is important to analyse your purchases, or payments, to keep

	Receipts				Payments		
Date	Description	£	p	Date	Description	£	p

Figure 7.1 Basic book-keeping system

track at regular intervals, and particularly year on year, of your outgoings. Without this analysis, you would not know, for example, how much your fuel bills had increased.

A basic loose-leaf accounts system has advantages for a new business. It is worth making a visit to a shop which specializes in this type of business stationery and studying the options. There are some well-known brand names in this area. Decide what you want your account sheets to do, and find the most appropriate ones for the job.

For the main record keeping, a standard 297 × 356 millimetres (11¾ by 14 inches) sheet with four columns for receipts and 16 columns for payments would probably be suitable.

It is useful to insert a folio number, such as a page number, and line number (01/01 for the first line of the first page). If these numbers are entered into invoices/receipts, it makes for an easier audit trail.

▶ Payment entries

A basic loose-leaf accounts layout could look something like the example in Figure 7.2.

A typical payment entry made by cheque or BACS would show, apart from the date and who was being paid, the gross amount in the Total Banked column (column 1), the amount of VAT (column 3), with the net amount in the appropriate analysis column (columns 4–16). If there was no VAT involved, the amount in the analysis column would be the same as that in the Total Banked column.

It is sometimes possible that items in one transaction apply to more than one analysis column. In this case, enter the amounts in the appropriate columns, and check to see that everything adds across to the figure in the Total Banked column (column 1).

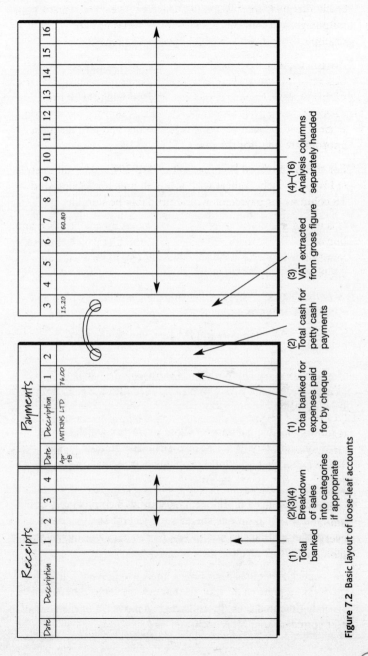

Figure 7.2 Basic layout of loose-leaf accounts

Receipts

Date	Description	1	2	3	4

Payments

Date	Description	1	2
Apr 18	MITKINS LTD	76.00	

3	4	5	6	7	8	9	10	11	12	13	14	15	16
15.20				60.80									

(1) Total banked

(2)(3)(4) Breakdown of sales into categories if appropriate

(1) Total banked for expenses paid for by cheque

(2) Total cash for petty cash payments

(3) VAT extracted from gross figure

(4)–(16) Analysis columns separately headed

A suitable breakdown of payments could be as follows, with each heading having its own column across the page:

- materials
- light/heat
- petrol/travel
- vehicle expenses
- telephone and postage
- printing and stationery
- entertainment
- subsistence/hotel
- capital equipment
- advertising
- rent/rates
- insurances.

It would also be useful to segregate out payments like:

- bank charges and interest (suggested column heading Bank Charges)
- money withdrawn from the bank for petty cash replenishment (Petty Cash)
- Department of Works & Pensions deductions (DWP) – i.e. National Insurance payments
- tax and VAT payments to HM Revenue & Customs (HMRC).

Another necessary column would show any drawings or directors' fees made from the business account for personal use (drawings/fees).

One indispensable column for those payments which for one reason or another will not fit into any other column is one headed Sundries, and would probably be the final one on the sheet.

If you find you need more headings than will comfortably fit into columns 4–16 on one sheet, use a second analysis sheet. Ask your accountant to advise you on the headings most appropriate to your business.

Cross-check all figures each time a sheet is completed. It is worth taking time to do this, so that any errors in calculation can be highlighted quickly, and you can move on to the new sheet confident that all is accurate.

As well as totalling each sheet as it is completed, the sheets should be ruled off, totalled and checked at suitable intervals – weekly, monthly, quarterly – depending on what is most appropriate for your business.

SALES

As supplementary sheets for recording sales or petty cash, a standard 297 × 210 millimetre (11¾ × 8¼ inch) sheet with four or five columns would enable you to record the facts needed.

For example, for invoiced sales:

Invoiced Sales			(1)	(2)	(3)	(4)
Date	Description	INV.	Gross	VAT	Net	Payment received
MAR 21	DEGEMA LTD	3821	702.53	140.50	562.03	MAY 8

Figure 7.3 Invoiced sales sheet

Having a Payment Received column (column 4) enables you to see at a glance how many outstanding invoices there are at any one time.

If your business is involved in cash sales, you would probably find it easier and more convenient to keep a separate record sheet for those. This is particularly important for retail outlets and eating establishments, where a mixture of payment methods includes cash, cheques and credit cards. A computerized system linked to your till is best for this.

PETTY CASH

Petty cash is a sum of money used for small, everyday expense items. These day-to-day business expenses need to be properly recorded.

A petty cash record could be as straightforward as this:

Petty Cash Record			(1) IN	(2) OUT	(3) Balance	(4)
Date	Description	Week no.				
	Opening balance		25.00	–	25.00	
w/e MAR 6	Expenses	①		6.10	18.90	
w/e MAR 13	Expenses	②		12.19	6.71	
MAR 21	Replenishment		50.00		56.71	

Figure 7.4 Petty cash record

It is, as you can see, a control or summary sheet. It is a very useful way of keeping an eye on the balance, to know when the petty cash float needs replenishing.

If it suits the pattern of your business, for both your sales and petty cash sheets you could rule them off each month. Apart from anything else, it means that if the figures do not balance, there is only one month's work to check!

It's a good, practical idea to have a small 160 × 100 millimetre (6 × 4 inch) cash book, which is easy to carry about, in which to record expenses as they happen. It is a very useful habit to get into. For example, when you buy the train ticket with cash, or the supply of postage stamps, write the amount in your petty cash book straight away, and carefully enclose the receipts: taxi drivers will usually give you a receipt if you ask for one.

At the end of, say, each week, the details of the expenses in your petty cash book are recorded on the main account sheet, with the total figure of each expenditure being written in the Total Cash column (column 2) with any VAT in column 3 and the net figures in the appropriate column analysis column (columns 4–16).

The total amount of the weekly expenditure is recorded on the petty cash record sheet. This is best done when the money is actually paid out: it also provides a good opportunity to check the balance in the petty cash tin.

When the money has been reclaimed, the petty cash book should be marked accordingly. Simply writing 'Reimbursed' across the entries in red ink could be sufficient.

Try to maintain a system to ensure that each expense claim is accompanied by a receipt. This is not possible in all cases, of course; parking meters will not issue a receipt (even though traffic wardens could provide another type of document in certain circumstances!) but a pay and display and multi-storey car park will provide a receipt. You can get a receipt for train tickets and the post office clerk will give you a receipt for your stamps if asked: complications can arise in a restaurant if a group of you wish to have separate bills for your own account records – try mentioning this fact when ordering your meal.

If something is bought for cash in a retail shop as a petty cash expense, it is important that the receipt shows the VAT number of that business. Many, though not all, till receipts show the VAT number of the business issuing it. It is always worth checking, and if there is no number, ask for a VAT receipt.

VAT (VALUE ADDED TAX)

VAT is the tax on goods and services as supplied. It is administered on behalf of the government by HMRC. We are concerned here about recording VAT in the books of the business. Even if you are not registered for VAT yourself, it could still be worthwhile isolating the VAT from your payments, because it may be possible to claim some of it in retrospect when you register; ask your accountant's advice on this. In any case, it is all good practice and a useful habit to get into.

You, as a business, can only be charged VAT by another organization if that business is itself VAT-registered. A VAT-registered company must show its nine-digit VAT registration number (set out like this: 987 6543 21) on its stationery, particularly its invoices and receipts. The point is that a VAT-registered company can claim back the VAT it has paid on legitimate business expenses.

VAT returns are made quarterly to HMRC. On your VAT Return form you fill in the value of the supplies you have made and received during the tax period, and pay the total tax you owe to HM Revenue & Customs, or claim a repayment if tax is owed to you (which can happen if your expenses have been greater than your receipts).

The VAT Return, and any payment due, must reach HMRC by the due date shown on the Return: penalties could be incurred for late payment, particularly if this is consistently happening.

The following extracts from notes supplied by HMRC may provide you with some helpful general background information about VAT:

▶ It is the person, not the business, who is registered for VAT. Each registration covers all the business activities of the registered person.

- The person to be registered can be a sole proprietor, a partnership (including husband and wife partnerships), a limited partnership, a limited company, a club or association, or a charity.

- If you are a taxable person, you must account for VAT whenever you make a taxable supply. The supply is your output and the VAT is your output tax.

- If your customer is registered for VAT and the supply is for the purposes of business, the supply is his input and the tax you charge him is his input tax. In the same way, VAT charged to you on your business purchases is your input tax.

Sources of help

There are many helpful leaflets describing the various aspects of VAT published by HMRC. It is worthwhile paying a visit to your local VAT office – addresses are in the phone book under 'Customs and Excise'.

All your dealings should be with your local VAT office; you only deal with the Head Office at Southend when you send them back your quarterly Return.

YEAR END

At the end of your company's financial year, you will have to submit all your books and accounts to your accountant to audit and present to HMRC. You will not be able to do this until the final bank statement for the year has arrived and been included in your accounts for that year.

If yours is a limited company, remember that the accounts must be submitted to Companies House not later than ten months after the end of the financial year, so it helps your accountant if you are prompt in completing and delivering the year's books or computer printouts.

MANUAL OR ELECTRONIC?

Doing the books manually could be the best way to start for a short time.

As your business progresses and expands, you may well consider computerizing its systems – take your accountant's advice before you embark on anything definite.

The sort of thing which might be suitable to consider is an accounts package on a desktop or laptop. Systems vary in sophistication. You can get systems which for your sales you key in the amount of goods supplied and details about price, settlement terms, VAT rates and so on and the system will do all the calculations for you, print out an invoice and add the required amount to your VAT Return at the end of the quarter.

For purchases, again you key in the details of the purchase and how payment is to be made; the system will produce a list of cheques to be made out (sometimes the cheques themselves). The amount of VAT you can claim will be automatically added to your VAT Return. The total of your net sales and purchases is then added as the actual figures on your cash flow forecast so that you can see at a glance how well your business is doing.

Do not rush into buying computer software for your book-keeping, particularly if you are fairly new to computers. You need to buy the software which is right for your business. You might decide in the end to computerize only part of it.

There are many different software packages on the market today that deal with basic accounts information and are easy to use. The most common and easily available are Sage and Quickbooks. The advantages of using one of these packages is that they have good telephone helplines and most accountants are familiar with them.

Make sure that you keep computerized records carefully. Make back-up copies in case your desktop or laptop becomes corrupted. Your accountant will need your summary printouts (which can usually be generated automatically by the system) for the audit trail. HMRC might require these as well.

If you are running a business with many customer accounts requiring lots of invoices each month, a computerized book-keeping system could save you a lot of time. If you are running say, a consultancy with far fewer invoices and payments, the amount of time saved is minimal.

The other type of package which you might find very useful is payroll software. Once set up, this can, with a minimal amount of keying in, generate payslips and cheques or BACS payments, so that you know your employees receive all the information and money to which they are entitled (see Chapter 9).

You might consider employing a professional book-keeper to do your books, make your VAT returns and run your wages system. These professionals often run small businesses themselves, and are usually trained in using the latest computerized package.

Your business bank account

A new business needs to have its own bank account; it is important to keep your personal and business finances separate. You can do this either traditionally through your high-street bank or electronically. Most banks now offer a free, secure online banking service. Once the online registration is completed, you should be able to view your bank balances and transactions, manage your standing orders and direct debits, pay bills, transfer money between your accounts and print statements. This could be more convenient than visiting the High Street, as you can access the sites 24 hours a day.

Whichever method of banking you choose, there are a few basic things to be considered and arranged:

▶ You can have a cashpoint card with a business account.

▶ You will need to provide a sum of money to deposit into the account to make it active (this would be recorded on the account sheets as 'capital introduced').

▶ If there is to be more than one signatory, arrangements should be made with the bank about whether all should sign or whether any one or two of those designated is sufficient. In any case, sample signatures from all signatories will need to be provided.

▶ You will receive a bank statement each month. You may have to ask for this because banks will sometimes only send statements quarterly, particularly for private accounts. This is too long a period for a business account.

▶ Consider whether you need to have an overdraft facility attached to this account. Find out what the arrangement fee will be, and how long the arrangement is to last before it is reviewed; negotiate for as long a period as possible.

▶ The name of the bank account needs to be decided. Will it be in the name of the business only, or perhaps in the name of the sole trader? Will it have the name of the person and the business name, for instance Arthur Cosford t/a Arco Services?

▶ A paying-in book will be necessary for depositing cheques and moneys received by the business.

A business bank account is bound to attract bank charges, even if it is only after a charge-free period, which some banks advertise for new business accounts. There should be a column to record these on the account analysis sheets. The monthly service charge shown on the statement is based on various receipts and payments handled during that month, and will, no doubt, also include a monthly accounts maintenance fee; these transactions are detailed separately. Business accounts can also include a net credit interest amount based on the balance held in your account, which should also be recorded on the account sheets under receipts. These are matters worth checking with the bank when you are considering opening a business account with them.

Consider whether you need to open a deposit account, where moneys not immediately needed could be placed to earn some interest. This, or any other suitable form of interest-earning account, could be useful for putting aside moneys in anticipation of the next VAT Return. Remember, if you charge VAT on your goods or supplies, a proportion of the money you receive will be required by HMRC. Beware of thinking you are better off than you really are and unwittingly spending your VAT money. Never use your VAT money for any other expenditure; HMRC is very good at retrieving what is its due. Remember, too, that you need to earmark money for your forthcoming tax bill.

BANK STATEMENTS

When you receive a bank statement for your business account, you need to check the details against the entries on your accounts sheets. This need not be a complicated exercise; simply tick (in red so that it will show up easily) the statement and the equivalent entry in your accounts sheets. Keep each statement carefully with your records; your accountant will need them when auditing your books.

You may well find items on the bank statement which you have not recorded on your account sheets. The bank charges and/or interest will probably be one. In this case, write the amount on the accounts sheet and tick both this entry and the statement. It can be useful to include in the entry on the accounts sheets the statement number where the charges/interest appeared; this could well help your accountant reconcile the figures at some future date.

Remember this: 'Will this make sense?'

This is quite a useful general principle to follow when doing the books: ask yourself when writing in a transaction, 'Will this make sense to somebody looking at it sometime in the future?' (your accountant, the VAT officer, HMRC). If there is any doubt at all, make a little note as a reminder – it could save you a grilling from any of the above-mentioned parties, with you racking your brains trying to remember the details or circumstances.

Other items on a business bank statement which have not been recorded on your accounts sheets could be direct debit deductions – for instance DWP Insurance. These can vary in amount, depending on the number of weeks in the month covered by the statement. As before, write the details on your accounts sheets – allocate a separate column to record these outgoings – tick them, and note the statement number on the accounts sheet for future reference.

Which system you use depends on your business, but answering these questions should help you make some fundamental decisions:

▶ Are you going to do the books yourself, or employ a book-keeper?

▶ Will you use a manual or computerized system?

▶ If computerized, which package will you use?

▶ Will you become VAT-registered? (If your annual turnover is £81,000 (2014/15 figure) you must register, but many companies register straight away so they can claim VAT back on their purchases.)

▶ Have you bought any accounting stationery you need?

▶ Have you set up a petty cash system?

▶ Have you opened a business bank account?

▶ Have you established a routine for doing the books, even if it is only passing on information to your book-keeper?

▶ Have you devised a system for storing your records once the end-of-year procedures have been completed? It's a legal requirement to keep the following records for seven years:

▷ Accounting sheets and ancillary documents

▷ Computer audit trails

▷ Receipts for payments made

▷ Copies of sales invoices

▷ VAT records, including Returns

▷ Bank statements

Insurance and personal finance

INSURANCE

Another decision you need to make early on is what insurance you are going to take out, which can be a substantial part of your expenditure but is allowable for tax purposes. This section lists the different insurances you can consider. The description of each is quite short because of the great variety of small businesses and insurance providers. Insurance brokers can be very helpful, but will charge a fee or commission.

▶ Premises

If you work from home, this will come under your general household insurance. You need not state that the house is partly used for business because clients and customers do not come to you. James and his garden landscape business is a good example.

If you own business premises, you will need to insure these premises, preferably through an insurance company that specializes in commercial property. If you rent business premises, check what your landlord's insurance covers. Sam, who runs her Affordable Fashion boutique, needs to know whether she is covered for fire, water damage, etc. Even if you rent just a garage for storing your business vehicles, check what the landlord's insurance covers. The information should be in your rental agreement.

Fixtures and fittings usually come under premises insurance, but may need to be separately insured if they are special to your business – for example fixed display stands or warehouse shelving.

▶ Contents

If you work from home your contents insurance will cover such things as desks and chairs, but it is wise to enumerate and describe expensive items such as computer equipment and specialist tools.

Where you own or rent premises, contents insurance is your responsibility. Contents include all equipment such as computers, cooking equipment, office furniture and a wide variety of things you would need to replace if the premises were destroyed. Remember to include all stock items, stored items and items ready for delivery.

▶ Mortgage protection

If your premises are mortgaged, what happens if you cannot meet the repayments for a month or two, or longer? Depending on the amount of the mortgage, and therefore repayments, a mortgage protection policy might be worth considering.

▶ Vehicles

All business vehicles must be insured for business use – without your insurance certificate and your MOT certificate, where necessary, you will not be able to purchase your tax disc.

If you use your own vehicle for business purposes, you should declare this when arranging your insurance. If you do not, you cannot claim for the loss of deliveries you are making, tools and equipment you carry around and so on. Interestingly, actors often have to pay heavy insurance premiums, as they are thought to transport other expensive actors!

▶ Goods in transit

If your business includes importing supplies, such as raw materials for a manufacturing process, special items for specific cuisines, or glassware and china for home decoration purposes, you need to be sure that your goods are insured until they reach your doorstep.

▶ Public liability

For certain businesses, where clients or customers come to you, public liability insurance (including against members of the public being injured while on your premises) is a must. However, if you go to other people in their houses, as James does, check whether this insurance is necessary or desirable for you. What if James drops a paving slab on somebody's foot?

▶ Employers' liability

If you employ people you are legally required to take out this insurance, to cover against injury or harm to your employees, as opposed to the general public. You must display your certificate where your employees can see it.

▶ Personal safety

Builders, decorators, arborists, window cleaners and people who work at heights need personal safety insurance. Householders are entitled to see your insurance certificate before they allow you to work on their premises. There are sometimes restrictions on the height at which you may work – not above the second floor of a house when decorating outside, for example.

▶ Travel

If you travel outside the UK in the course of your business, you may be required to provide proof of travel insurance. People who work on cruise ships, for example, are normally required by the cruise line to have this type of cover. Travel insurance premiums can increase considerably as you get older, just because of your age; look for an insurance company which charges you on your health record, if that seems more appropriate.

▶ Health

It is worth thinking about insuring against loss of earnings through ill health, particularly if yours is a very small business, which depends entirely on one or two people. Being self-employed means you will not be paid Statutory Sick Pay; in other words: no work, no income. As mentioned in Chapter 1 a regular check-up is a good form of insurance, but it cannot predict your breaking your leg, making you unable to drive.

▶ Professional indemnity

This insurance can be extremely costly. It covers you against claims for injury or negligence and is usually required for professional people such as chiropodists, solicitors, dentists, accountants, book-keepers, healing practitioners and even, on occasion, trainers.

▶ Life

What happens when you die, if you are still in business? If you are in partnership that partnership ceases automatically when a partner dies. So, as well as life insurance for your family's peace of mind, it is worth exploring insurance which would enable your other partner or partners to continue the business.

It is worth checking with your professional or trade association which insurances are essential for your type of business. These bodies can also help you find the right insurance provider. Being self-employed is a risky business!

PERSONAL FINANCE

First, a caveat: the information in this chapter is liable to change, so check on the up-to-date position. Listen to the Chancellor of the Exchequer's budget speech and read the small print.

Your personal finances change when you become self-employed, so you have to make sure these are well organized. You no longer have a salary or wage paid to you, you have to finance your personal life, and that of your family, perhaps, from your business, and also pay your National Insurance contributions and income tax and make your own pension arrangements.

MONEY FOR PERSONAL USE

You will need money for personal use. You still need to pay your household bills, and pay for food and clothing, presents, holidays and all the other personal things you do, including driving for social reasons. As a sole trader or a member of a partnership, you can either do this regularly, say monthly, or on an as-and-when basis; this withdrawal of money from the business is classed as 'Drawings'. If you are a limited company director, you are more likely to withdraw a regular amount in the form of a director's salary or fees, and then a dividend at the end of the year.

It is important to distinguish between business and personal expenditure. If in doubt, ask yourself, 'Am I doing this for business reasons only?' If the answer is 'yes', then it is obviously a business expense. The last section in this chapter, Allowable business expenses, includes a list of expenses you should be able to claim for tax purposes, but – as ever – seek your accountant's advice. You may, for example, think you can claim the VAT back on a new vehicle. Not so, unfortunately.

NATIONAL INSURANCE CONTRIBUTIONS AND PENSIONS

Almost everybody who is self-employed pays towards a basic state pension through making National Insurance (NI) contributions. Earlier in the chapter, we showed you how you would record these on your accounts sheets if you are paying by direct debit. There are numerous methods of payment – ask the DWP for details.

The amount you have to pay depends partly on the amount of your taxable business profit. Most self-employed individuals have to pay Class 2 contributions. Above a certain profit level individuals must pay Class 4 contributions. Some is paid by monthly contributions and some is paid at the same time as your income tax. Ask your accountant for details.

If you are self-employed, you can get tax relief on payments to a personal pension plan (PPP). This is one of the best forms of investment you can make. Do your pension sums well ahead of retirement: once your pension starts to be paid, you will not be able to take a cash lump sum.

INCOME TAX

To be treated as self-employed for tax purposes, you must convince your tax office (preferably through your accountant) that you are genuinely in business on your own account, and not an employee. This will depend, among other things, on whether you risk your own money or provide major items of equipment, whether you are told what to do, where, when and how – or decide by yourself.

Each local office of HMRC and the DWP has someone responsible for saying whether or not you will be treated as self-employed.

If you form a limited company, the tax rules are quite different; you pay corporation tax on the business profits, and you will need the help of your accountant to deal with this.

Sole traders and partnerships are taxed in a similar way, but there are special rules for partnerships. In a partnership the partners are each responsible for the tax on their own income not related to the partnership. The partnership also gets its own tax return. The profit is then divided between the individual partners in proportion to what each gets under the partnership agreement. Each partner's share is taxed at his or her own rate of tax, taking into account other personal income and allowances.

As a self-employed person you will need to complete a self-assessment tax return. Self-employed people have to assess their tax liability on the current year's income, and pay the year's tax in two instalments. Your accountant will advise you on what you should do, and there is a range of leaflets available from HMRC and advice on their website.

It is important to sort out your arrangements for self-assessment, because the Inspector of Taxes can audit anyone's return and books at any time. Be sure to keep records of all your transactions – you could be fined if you do not.

Allowable business expenses

You can deduct allowable business expenses from your profits. An expense will be allowable only if it is incurred 'wholly and exclusively' for the business. This does not mean that you can claim nothing if, for example, you use your car partly for business and partly for private purposes, or use part of your home for business.

You can normally claim the proportion of these costs that is attributable to business use – you will have to agree the proportion with your tax office (preferably via your accountant).

Car expenses are usually shared out according to mileage.

If you are self-employed (or have some freelance or spare-time work) and do part of your work at home, you can normally claim, as an allowable expense, the proportion of the cost of running your home attributable to business use. You will have to agree with your tax office – through your accountant – what proportion of telephone, heating bills, etc. you can claim.

If you devote part of your home, a room, say, exclusively to business use, you may be able to claim a proportion of rent and council tax – usually based on the number and size of rooms. HOWEVER, exclusive use for business purposes may mean some capital gains tax to pay when you sell your house – check with your accountant.

Circumstances vary considerably, but the sort of business expenses which might be allowable – or not allowable – could be:

► **Basic costs and general running expenses**

▷ *Normally allowed:* Cost of goods bought for resale and raw materials; advertising; delivery charges; heating and lighting; cleaning; rates and rent of business premises; telephone and postage; replacement of small tools and special clothing; stationery; relevant books and magazines; accountant's fees; bank charges on business accounts; subscriptions to professional and trade organizations; use of home for work: proportion of telephone, lighting, heating, cleaning, insurance, proportion of rent and rates if part of home is used exclusively for business (but beware of capital gains tax).

▷ *Not allowed:* Initial cost of machinery; vehicles; equipment; permanent advertising signs.

► **Capital expenditure and depreciation**

▷ *Not allowed:* Capital expenditure (i.e. what you spend on buying cars, machinery, etc.) is not an allowable expense; depreciation of equipment (this would be dealt with by your accountant under Capital Allowances).

▶ **Entertaining**

▷ *Normally allowed:* Entertainment of your staff: ex gratia payments not paid in lieu of wages; a modest expenditure (about £150 per employee to include partners) is allowed for Christmas or other annual entertainment.

▷ *Not allowed:* Any business entertaining.

▶ **Gifts**

▷ *Normally allowed:* Gifts so long as the gift advertises your business.

▷ *Not allowed:* Food, drink, tobacco gifts or vouchers for goods given to anyone other than employees.

▶ **Hiring**

▷ *Normally allowed:* Reasonable charge for hire of capital goods, including cars.

▶ **Insurance**

▷ *Normally allowed:* Business insurance premiums – e.g. employers' liability; fire and theft; motor; employees' life cover.

▷ *Not allowed:* Premiums for your own life insurance; accident insurance; sickness insurance.

▶ **Interest payments**

▷ *Normally allowed:* Interest on, and costs of arranging overdrafts and loans for business purposes.

▷ *Not allowed:* Interest on capital paid or credited to partners; interest on overdue tax.

▶ **Legal costs**

▷ *Normally allowed:* Cost of recovering debts; defending business rights; preparing service agreements; appealing against rates on business premises; renewing lease, with landlord's consent, for 50 years or less (but not if premium paid).

▷ *Not allowed:* Expenses (including stamp duty) for acquiring land, buildings or leases; fines and other penalties for breaking the law; costs of fighting a tax case.

► **Patents, designs and trade marks**

▷ *Normally allowed:* Trade marks, designs and patents: fees paid to register trade mark or design, or to obtain a patent.

▷ *Not allowed:* Cost of buying patent.

► **Repairs**

▷ *Normally allowed:* Normal repairs and maintenance to premises and equipment.

▷ *Not allowed:* Costs of additions, alterations or improvements.

► **Subscriptions/contributions**

▷ *Normally allowed:* Payments which secure benefits for your business and staff; payments to professional bodies which have arrangements with HM Revenue & Customs (in some cases only a proportion of the payment can be claimed).

▷ *Not allowed:* Payments to political parties; places of worship; charities (small gifts to local charities may be allowable).

► **Tax and National Insurance**

▷ *Normally allowed:* Employers' National Insurance contributions for employees; VAT on allowable business expenses if you are a VAT-registered trader.

▷ *Not allowed:* income tax; capital gains tax; inheritance tax; your own National Insurance contributions.

► **Travelling and subsistence**

▷ *Normally allowed:* Cost of travel and accommodation on business trips; reasonable cost of dinner and breakfast – but not lunch – on overnight trips; travel between different places of work; running costs of own car – whole of cost, excluding depreciation if used privately, too.

▷ *Not allowed:* Travel between home and business; cost of buying car or van.

▶ **Wages and salaries**

▷ *Normally allowed:* Wages, salaries, redundancy and reasonable leaving payments paid to employees; pensions for ex-employees and their dependants; training costs for employees to acquire or improve skills needed for their current job, and re-training costs for employees who are leaving.

▷ *Not allowed:* Your own wages or salary or that of any partner.

Try it now: Allowable expenses

Read each item and decide, without looking at the list above if you can, whether that item is allowable, partly allowable or not allowable for business expenses. If you gradually learn what you can and cannot claim, it will make life much easier for you and your accountant.

✳ Your own drawings or director's salary
✳ Travel between your home and place of work
✳ Accountant's fees
✳ Lighting and heating when working from home
✳ Travel and accommodation on business trips
✳ Subscriptions to professional bodies
✳ Capital expenditure
✳ Your own accident insurance
✳ Gifts given to employees
✳ Training costs
✳ Costs of alterations and improvements to your premises
✳ Pension payments

Now check with the list and see how well you did. It is complicated and very liable to change, so check on the up-to-date position every year.

If you have any doubts about this, you know who to turn to – your accountant. If he or she gets it badly wrong, you can sue, and hope his or her professional indemnity Insurance is up to date!

Focus points

✻ Setting up good systems for your business and personal finances takes time, but it is worth doing it early on in your new business life.

✻ Do employ a good accountant and follow his or her advice on doing the books, banking, insurance, your finances and allowable business expenditure.

Next step

This particular next step is often an early step in your new business life. Administration needs to be done from the start, so you need somewhere to do it, whether you work from home or rent or own other premises. The next chapter asks you to make decisions about your office, its furniture, its equipment and its stationery. It also gives advice on health and safety in the office, for both you and any employees.

The office

In this chapter you will learn:

▶ *How to set up an efficient, pleasant working environment*

▶ *How to choose which furniture and equipment you will need for your office, from desks and photocopiers to hole punchers*

▶ *How to choose what kind of IT you will need – both hardware and software*

▶ *How to develop professional-looking stationery, from labels and envelopes to invoices and statements of account.*

Whatever your business, you need an 'office', even if it is only the corner of your dining table. It may start off there, as many small businesses do, but you'll soon find you need more space than that, and the rest of the household will welcome your moving off the table.

? Self-assessment: Think about your own office

1 Where is it going to be?

2 What furniture are you likely to need?

3 What office equipment will you need?

4 Which contact methods will your clients or customers be able to use? Mobile, email, fax, Facebook, Twitter, what?

5 What does HASAWA stand for?

6 What stationery are you likely to need?

7 Which details must be on an invoice?

8 What is a remittance advice?

9 How would the Offices, Shops and Railway Premises Act 1963 apply to you?

10 Who is going to do your office work?

If you are working from home, a separate room as a study or office is ideal. For one thing you can be reasonably quiet and able to concentrate; for another, you can shut the door at the end of your working day.

You may well be renting premises, in which case you will need a small space where you, or somebody else, can do all the paperwork and computer work which goes with your business. Sam in her Affordable Fashion boutique, for example, will need somewhere out of sight of the customers to prepare her banking, do her ordering, pay her suppliers, and do all the other bits and pieces she needs to do on a regular basis behind the scenes. James, on the other hand, with his gardening consultancy, will need space at home for drawing designs and, again, attending to the routine office work. He might even have a shed in the garden, provided there is enough heat and light: he, of all people, would know how to manage that.

Your business might itself be office based, particularly if you are working with a partner or other directors outside the family. This will help you keep your business and your domestic life separate. Sole proprietors who are, say, book-keepers, accountants or trainers could probably work from home and visit clients' premises. But people such as solicitors, design consultants or printers, where their clients come to them, certainly need good office premises, usually with a reception area, as a fundamental part of their business.

Some craftspeople work from home, others rent workshops, perhaps in a craft centre. Manufacturers need space in which to make their products. Both need office space somewhere, decent office space where people can work comfortably and efficiently. Office work is not particularly energetic – more brain power than muscle power – so people who work in offices need good heating and lighting, and air conditioning if necessary. It is difficult to operate a keyboard with cold fingers.

Furniture and equipment

FURNITURE

You can manage with very little purpose-built furniture to start with, but you should try to keep all your business documentation separate from your general household paperwork, if you are working from home. You will find that you very soon need, at least, the following:

▶ **Files** in which to keep correspondence, copy invoices, etc.

▶ **Somewhere to keep the files** – probably a two-drawer cabinet will do to start with.

▶ **Somewhere to store your stationery** – desk drawers or a small cupboard are better than filing cabinet drawers. You may be aiming for a paperless office, which is quite possible. If so, set this up right from the start and make sure your computer files are well named and easy to find.

▶ A **table** or **desk** for your desktop or laptop – make sure it is big enough to take the desktop and the papers you are working from.

▶ A **chair** of the right height for writing or keying. It may not be you who does the writing or keying, but whoever does it needs a desk or table, and chair of the right height. This is very important because working for any length of time at the wrong height can cause backache, wrist ache, and all sorts of other aches and pains. It is worth getting an adjustable typing chair with good back support.

There is usually a second-hand office furniture shop not too far away from which you can get your basic furniture. Sometimes you can be lucky and hear of a large office which is being refurbished and needs to get rid of its out-of-date furniture. This can be quite prestigious furniture, but if you are working from home, make sure it will fit in! If your business requires prestigious-looking furniture from the start, remember to include the cost in your business plan.

Some businesses need a small meeting place in their office premises for internal meetings with members of the team, and for external meetings with clients or customers and suppliers. This space needs to be private so that confidential matters can be discussed without fear of interruption. Whether this space is part of your office or a separate room, you will need a table and three or four chairs. Round tables are good for discussion, but it depends what fits; the table can also be used for collating papers or studying printouts – your own desk is often too small or too cluttered to be able to do this properly. Keep this table clear, if you can: visitors will think it looks organized and business-like.

EQUIPMENT

The main items of equipment you may need are: photocopier; desktop; laptop; tablet; printer; telephone; franking machine; desk lamp; safe; waste bin; fireproof/smoke-proof box for valuable data – supported by smaller, but important items such as: stapler and staples; staple remover; date stamp; hole puncher; guillotine; paper clips; adhesive tape; scissors.

▶ Franking machine

If your postal output is sufficient to warrant it, you could use a franking machine. If you are a franking machine user, you have to:

- obtain authority from the Post Office before starting to use a machine

- pay in advance for postage at a specified post office

- follow the local conditions about how to face and bundle franked mail

- return a completed control card to the Post Office at the close of business each working week

- use a machine authorized by the Post Office and have it regularly maintained.

▶ Photocopier

After a telephone and desktop or laptop, a good photocopier is probably the next important item of equipment. Get as good a one as you can afford. These are some of the features to look out for:

- automatic sheet feed

- double-sided copying

- collator

- reduction and enlargement

- memory for reduction and enlargement

- two-page separation, for copying pages of books or magazines (but watch the copyright laws) and A3 masters as two separate A4 sheets.

Large suppliers are always willing to lease you a photocopier, with an integrated maintenance agreement. This can be advantageous from the accounting point of view (ask your accountant) and very important if your copier is going to get heavy wear – it is the one item of office equipment which always seems to be jamming or breaking down. If you lease, you have to remember that you pay a charge every time you press the button, as well as your quarterly leasing bill.

If you buy a copier outright, you have no leasing charges, but you might spend a lot in maintenance. It is possible to get a maintenance agreement for copiers which are owned – ask the manufacturers how to go about this. There is a second-hand market in photocopiers, but you usually do not know how they have been used or misused.

There are plenty of photocopier paper suppliers around, but if you use inferior paper you can find that it never stops jamming or takes through two sheets at a time. It is worth considering using the paper sold, or at least recommended, by the suppliers.

Photocopiers can be a multi-purpose machine, doing your photocopying, scanning, printing and faxing if you need it. As with any multi-purpose machine, it is a good idea to decide right from the start exactly what you want the machine to do, and then buy or lease the best machine you can afford.

Try it now: Your office furniture and equipment

Furnish and equip your office space. Using this list of furniture and equipment, write down which item you need and how many. Some items you will not need at all. If your office is just the corner of the kitchen table, this list may seem laughable, but you will almost certainly need some of the equipment. Bear in mind how much space you have, and how many people are going to work or meet in your office. Take into account, too, how many power points you have and where they are.

Furniture:

✳ Workstation	☐	✳ Chair	☐
✳ Desk	☐	✳ Filing cabinet	☐
✳ Table	☐	✳ Stationery store	☐

Equipment:

✳ Photocopier	☐	✳ Tablet	☐
✳ Franking machine	☐	✳ Desk lamp	☐
✳ Printer	☐	✳ Safe	☐
✳ Telephone	☐	✳ Waste bin	☐
✳ Desktop	☐	✳ Fire/smoke-proof	
✳ Laptop	☐	box	☐

Small items of equipment:

✳ Stapler and staples	☐	✳ Guillotine	☐
✳ Staple remover	☐	✳ Paper clips	☐
✳ Date stamp	☐	✳ Adhesive tape	☐
✳ Hole puncher	☐	✳ Scissors	☐

Computers

A desktop or laptop is a must for your business. Even if you are not computer literate yourself (and it takes time to learn how to use a computer to the best advantage), a family member, business partner or employee will expect to work with a good computer. Businesses are expected to be able to send and receive emails and have their own website, but make sure your system can cope with a variety of attachments. You may also work from a tablet, but if there is a lot of keying in to be done, the keyboard might be too small.

HARDWARE, SOFTWARE AND OTHER MATERIALS

What will you get in a personal computer package, and what can you use it for? You should get both hardware and software, as well as any associated materials.

▶ Hardware

This includes a keyboard, mouse, monitor, built-in CD drive and printer as well as the central processing unit (CPU) which makes the whole thing work.

The **keyboard** will be a normal QWERTY keyboard – so called because those are the first letters of the alpha keys on the top row – with extra function keys. Some will have a numeric keypad on the right, but you can always use the numbers on the top row of the keyboard proper. Remember to use the 0, not a capital 'O', for nought and a 1, not a small 'l' (ell), for one. Check that your keyboard has a euro (€) key or access to the symbol.

The **printer** is the key to the quality of output. Get as good a printer as you can afford. Colour printers enhance the quality of the output for proposals and other 'selling' documents, and are becoming a must for all businesses.

▶ The software

This comprises the computer programs, which allow you to control your computer and do things such as word processing, book-keeping and so on. You could get:

- a good **word-processing package**, for correspondence, reports, etc. WP software is sophisticated and will meet most documentation needs

- an **accounts package** for book-keeping

- a **spreadsheet package**, which you can use for doing cash flow forecasts, production forecasts, etc.

- a **spellchecker** for checking your spelling; they are not infallible because they often cannot cope with homonyms (their/there etc.) – this comes as part of the WP package

- a **'presentations' package** for creating graphs, slides, transparencies, etc.

- **communications software** which (with the aid of a modem or router) will allow you to access email, the Internet and, where appropriate, receive and send faxes.

Usually, these software packages are included with the hardware package you buy, but sometimes they come as extras. You need to check. If you are selling online (e-commerce), you may need additional software.

You always get at least one instruction manual, though some are still incomprehensible to non-computer people. Sometimes you find word-processing instructions which are 'idiot-proof' and accounting instructions which you cannot understand, all in the same manual. Again you need to check.

► The materials

As well as the system (hardware and software) you will need:

- **cables:** sometimes part of the package, sometimes extra

- **disks:** as well as disks which make your desktop work (called system, operator or program disks), which will probably come with the package, you will need some additional CDs or memory sticks on which to store or backup the work you do. There are two versions of these: CD-RW (ReWriteable, which means you can delete or overwrite the data); CD-R (Readable, which means the data is permanently burned into the disk and cannot be amended)

- **cartridges:** ink or toner, whichever is correct for the printer
- **paper:** for special applications such as database printouts. For general purposes normal paper will suffice.

There are lots of other 'extras' which you may or may not need. Look at a computer supplies catalogue if you want to see the sort of thing you can get. Remember anyway that you have to budget for at least the basics, which can cost quite a bit in both money and learning time.

COMPUTER SUPPLIERS

As with stationery, you can buy a desktop or laptop in many high-street shops, but it is worth going to a supplier who can advise you on what is best for you, and give you help when you need it initially. Computer manufacturers will usually be able to give you the name of the nearest supplier of their machines, and adverts for the packages are in almost every newspaper.

Take time to do some research before laying out capital on a desktop or laptop. Visiting an exhibition can be helpful, but try to go with someone who knows what to look for.

You might like to consider having a maintenance agreement for any of the larger systems. It is something to talk to your supplier about because you become very machine dependent and can lose a lot of business if your system stops working for any length of time.

WIRELESS

You may well want to consider going wireless from the start, which means you can have desktops, laptops, tablets and printers anywhere in your place of work – which might be in your house, in the garden shed or in rented office premises. You are not tied to power points if you have a laptop, though you will need a router and, if you already have a desktop, you may need a dongle (or wireless network adaptor).

You need to be aware of the security aspect of working wirelessly and always use a protected password, so that the neighbours or someone parked outside your house, for example, cannot access your system. Ask your IT expert's advice.

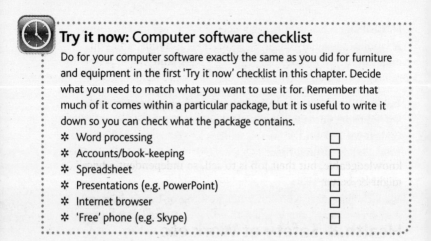

Try it now: Computer software checklist

Do for your computer software exactly the same as you did for furniture and equipment in the first 'Try it now' checklist in this chapter. Decide what you need to match what you want to use it for. Remember that much of it comes within a particular package, but it is useful to write it down so you can check what the package contains.

* Word processing ☐
* Accounts/book-keeping ☐
* Spreadsheet ☐
* Presentations (e.g. PowerPoint) ☐
* Internet browser ☐
* 'Free' phone (e.g. Skype) ☐

Remember this: 'GI = GO'

The old saying 'GI = GO' is still true. Garbage in does result in garbage out, so you need to be skilled in using your office equipment, or employ someone who is.

Telephones

There are so many ways of communicating using your mobile and landline that it is as well to set out early on, in conjunction with your computer decisions, exactly what you want to use them for. If you are new to the world of computers and telecommunications, it may be as well to stick to the simpler versions at first. You can always upgrade later on, but it is worth remembering two things:

1 It takes time to set these things up and to learn how to use them.

2 Every time you change your email address or a phone number, you may need to reprint your headed stationery, and amend your website and other online contact details.

There is a method of 'buying' your email address so you do not have to change it when you change your ISP.

LANDLINE

A landline is usually cheaper to run than a mobile, and you might need it for your desktop with broadband. Some people do not trust companies which give mobile phone numbers only.

When you have decided what you want your computer and telephone to do, you can start shopping around for the systems best suited to you. Get advice from someone who really knows what they are talking about: high-street sales people are usually knowledgeable, but their job is to sell, so independent advice might be better.

Health & Safety at Work etc. Act 1974 (HASAWA)

Many people forget that the Health & Safety at Work etc. Act 1974 (HASAWA) applies just as much in the office as it does in any other workplace. If you are on your own, health and safety in the office are important because you cannot afford to have accidents. If you are employing others, you have a legal obligation to make their working conditions healthy and safe.

DOS AND DON'TS

Health and safety in the office is really common sense, but there are a few DOs and DON'Ts:

▶ **Do**

▶ Make sure the electrical wiring is in good condition.

▶ Route wires and cables through a conduit.

▶ Have the right fire extinguishers handy and topped up – and know how to use them.

▶ Have sensible arrangements for making hot drinks.

▶ Observe the precautions for unjamming paper in the photocopier – some parts of the machine get very hot.

▶ Lift heavy items (e.g. boxes of paper) properly.

▶ Keep fire exits clear at all times.

- ▶ Know what to do in the event of a fire.

- ▶ Ensure that all staff know the fire drill.

▶ Don't

- ▶ Leave cabinet and cupboard doors open.

- ▶ Open more than one drawer of a filing cabinet at a time.

- ▶ Leave cables trailing.

- ▶ Leave piles of papers and files where people can trip over them.

- ▶ Let jewellery and ties or scarves dangle in moving parts of equipment.

- ▶ Carry things which are too heavy for you; get help, or use a trolley.

- ▶ Stand on chairs – use steps.

- ▶ Use adhesive sprays (like Spray Mount) in confined spaces without ventilation.

- ▶ Smoke – smoking in any public space is illegal.

WHAT ABOUT DESKTOPS AND LAPTOPS?

Prolonged use of desktops and laptops can cause many aches, pains and even permanent damage. There are various Health & Safety Executive (HSE) publications on this issue, giving the latest research findings, advice and guidance. Call the Health & Safety Executive Infoline on 0845 0055 or visit their website www.hse.gov.uk

▶ Eyestrain

People do complain of eyestrain and headaches after prolonged use of desktops and laptops, but there is no evidence that use damages the eyes. It is much more likely that spectacles are not worn when they are needed, or that incorrect spectacles are worn (bifocals can be a particular problem), or that workstation design and job content is at fault. Follow these guidelines:

1 Have your eyes tested by an optician.

2 Check the workstation design, particularly for glare.

3 Consider the job rotation and whether you are spending too long at the desktop or laptop without a break. This work is very concentrated, which in itself can cause stress and fatigue. The HSE recommend 10 minutes' break from the screen (i.e. doing something else) every hour.

DESIGN OF WORKSTATIONS

Badly designed workstations are the most likely cause of aches and pains. Check the following:

▶ There is sufficient space on the worktop, with document holders if required.

▶ The worktop is at the right height.

▶ The printer is at the right height.

▶ The chair is comfortable and adjustable for height and angle.

▶ Lighting is sufficient to illuminate surfaces from which work is being copied.

▶ Lighting is not directed straight on to the screen, whether it is sunlight or artificial light – it can cause glare.

▶ Ambient lighting is not too harsh.

▶ You have extra directional lighting for dull days and blinds for very sunny days.

▶ You have a comfortable working temperature.

▶ Use anti-static mats, sprays, etc. if necessary.

▶ A pleasing décor is helpful – if working towards a wall, make sure you look at something unobtrusive and restful.

▶ Do not work facing a window.

▶ Make sure you sit up straight with your back supported and with your hands at the right angle on the keyboard.

▶ Adjust the brightness of the screen to suit your requirements.

If you have employees working in your office, check with the Offices, Shops and Railway Premises Act 1963 that you have spaced the work stations out correctly.

Stationery

The stationery you are likely to need, depending on the nature of your business, is:

HEADED PAPER

In Chapter 3 you designed your headed paper. Most correspondence is done by email, but you will need a supply of headed paper for the occasional letter and possibly for invoices, statements and order forms, if these are not computerized. You will almost certainly need headed paper for estimates and quotations. Your headed paper should be at least 70 gsm weight, preferably 80 gsm; gsm stands for 'grams per square metre'.

You may prefer to have a ream (about 480 sheets) of plain paper and print your own letterhead on to it. Just occasionally, you might need a continuation sheet, which should be the same weight and colour as your headed paper, but without the letterhead. A continuation sheet on paper which is not the same weight and colour looks cheap.

PHOTOCOPYING PAPER

It is usually wise to use the paper recommended by the manufacturer, even though it is a little more expensive. Cheaper paper can keep jamming up.

You do not need to print out every email you send, but you may wish to keep a fair percentage of them to keep in a client's or customer's file, for example. If these printouts are for your own records, you can use the back of good, clean paper you have used to print out drafts and then amended. If you have a two-drawer photocopier, you can make drawer 1 the default drawer for scrap paper and drawer 2 the one with clean, unused paper. Make sure the paper is not wrinkled in any way; if it is, it is likely to jam. You can save many reams of paper by doing this: not only is it good for the environment, it is also good for your business expenditure.

ENVELOPES

You will probably need a small supply of good-quality envelopes the same weight and colour as your letterhead, but these should last you a long time. It depends how prestigious you want your envelope to look when it reaches its destination, bearing in mind who is likely to be opening it. A supply of manila or white envelopes for run-of-the-mill correspondence is useful, but it is acceptable to reuse envelopes of all sizes. Keep the good ones which you receive and reuse those, but remember to cross out and rewrite who it is from as well as who it is to, and you will need a new stamp. Keeping a supply of those return envelopes you receive with certain junk mail to hold your weekly petty cash receipts is a simple cost-saving exercise.

LABELS

These are useful for mailshots and for reusing envelopes. The bigger ones are better for people with long addresses. They are also useful for packages and parcels you have to send.

COMPLIMENTS SLIPS

The design and layout of these were discussed in Chapter 3. You can use your plain paper to print out three or four to an A4 page and guillotine them down.

BUSINESS CARDS

Again, you have already thought about the design and layout of these. You will need a good supply, particularly if your business is very new and you are doing a lot of networking. Get them printed on good card, small enough to go into a credit card holder. Make sure they are easy to read and contain all the necessary information. Some people like to leave the back blank; others like to use it to promote the various aspects of their business.

STATIONERY SUPPLIERS

You can get supplies of stationery from high-street shops, but a stationery supplier is often more economical. You will find these in *Yellow Pages* or your *Thomson Local*. What suppliers often do is to use a standard catalogue and fix their own prices; they sometimes have special offers on standard stationery such as photocopying paper, envelopes, toner cartridges, etc. There can be an enormous difference in price, delivery facilities and payment terms, so it is worth shopping around.

As a business, you can also use a cash-and-carry wholesaler such as Bookers or Staples, but of course they do not deliver. However, they are usually open until late at night and sometimes seven days a week. You might already be intending to buy from a cash-and-carry wholesaler, particularly if you run a small retail shop. If so, remember the office side (in the non-foods area) as well.

It is also worth searching the Internet: printer cartridges, in particular, are often perfectly OK, delivered the next day and cost a lot less. Make sure the cartridge, if not the manufacturer's own, is compatible with your printer and that your printer is not 'protected' so that it will work only with its own official manufacturer's cartridges.

Try it now: Stationery checklist

In the same way as you completed the first two 'Try it now' boxes, do the same for your stationery. Make a note, too, of how much you need to order to get you off the ground. One ream of paper is about 480 sheets (of A4).

* Headed paper   ☐
* Plain paper, good quality   ☐
* Photocopying paper   ☐
* Envelopes   ☐
* Labels   ☐
* Compliments slips   ☐
* Business cards   ☐

Finally, who will be your main stationery suppler?

Business documents

When you are laying out your business documents, make sure that each has all the information needed and, most important, the right name of the document. Call an 'estimate' a 'quotation', and you could land yourself in trouble. Always remember to include your company name, address, telephone number, email and website addresses on every document.

Different types of business need different documents, but here are descriptions and formats for the main ones. Look at the design and layout of the documents coming into your business; this will help with the layout and design of your own. Your software package may already have these documents ready for you to customize, or you can download free software from the Internet to help you.

ESTIMATE

Ordinary headed paper will do. This is an estimate, as it says, of how much the service will cost. An estimate is not necessarily the final price to be charged. It is often used by businesses like builders and decorators who do not know what they might uncover.

Remember to say that VAT is extra – for instance 'All charges subject to x% VAT.' 'E&OE' (Errors and Omissions Excepted) is often added at the bottom.

QUOTATION

Builders and decorators sometimes say that potential customers prefer quotations, because estimates are not a fixed price. Quotations need to be carefully costed. A quotation gives a firm price for the product or service, again usually net of VAT. The layout can be the same as for an estimate.

NEWCO

22 ELMHURST ROAD   HAWTON   NORTHANTS   NN7 4PX
TELEPHONE 01327 563418   FAX: 01327 563520   VAT REGISTRATION: 987 6543 21
E-MAIL NEWCO@AOL.COM   WWW.NOOCO.CO.UK

ESTIMATE

(today's date)

Mr R V Pugh
12 Ravens Close
Willington
Northants
NN7 6RL

      Estimate for redecorating outside of
        'Mountside' Hill Lane Andley

To: re-paint windows, doors and
     garden gate on the outside of
     the property in a colour to
     be selected.

               for the sum of   <u>£3,029</u>
                   plus VAT

Please note:

If our estimate is accepted, work will be
started in one month's time.

Figure 8.1 Example estimate

ORDER FORM

Affordable Fashion

21 Upper High Street
Andover
Hampshire
SP10 4ZU

Telephone: 01264 777888
Email: sam.afford@tiscali.com

ORDER

Date: (Today's date)

Order No: 100

To:
Quantock Fashions
Taunton Road
Bridgwater
Somerset
TA7 5DQ

Code	Description	Colour	Size	Quantity	Price each	Total price
QF024	Boot-strap trousers	Black	10	5	49.00	245.00
QF025	Boot-strap trousers	Black	12	5	49.00	245.00
QF026	Boot-strap trousers	Black	14	5	49.00	245.00
QF027	Boot-strap trousers	Black	16	3	54.00	162.00

Order Total:	**£897.00**

Sole Proprietor: Samantha Holdness

Figure 8.2 Example order form

If you need your customers to place written orders for your product or service, you can provide them with an order form. This will make sure that you get all the details you need to fulfil the order correctly. Do not forget VAT, postage and packing or carriage and discounts, if these are applicable. You can send out printed forms or you may wish to set up an order form on your website.

INVOICE

A printed or computer format is desirable, but it can be typed on headed paper. These are the details which should always appear on an invoice:

- ▶ Name and address of supplier
- ▶ Name and address of purchaser/customer
- ▶ Date
- ▶ Invoice number
- ▶ Order number (if applicable) or reference
- ▶ Quantity and description of goods (plus catalogue number if applicable) or service
- ▶ Unit price
- ▶ Total without VAT
- ▶ Discount (if applicable)
- ▶ Postage and packing, carriage (if applicable)
- ▶ Final net total
- ▶ Amount of VAT at appropriate percentage(s)
- ▶ Total including VAT
- ▶ VAT registration number
- ▶ Payment terms.

Note: VAT is added after all other calculations have been made.

Quantock Fashions Plc

Taunton Road   Bridgwater   Somerset   TA7 5DQ

Telephone: 01278 687422   Email: quantockfashions@aol.com   www.quantockfashions.co.uk

INVOICE

Date: (Today's date)   **Invoice No:** 48762

Order No: 100

To: Affordable Fashion
          21 Upper High Street
          Andover
          Hampshire
          SP10 4ZU

5 x Boot-strap trousers	QF024	Black	size 10	@ £49 each	245.00
5 x Boot-strap trousers	QF025	Black	size 12	@ £49 each	245.00
5 x Boot-strap trousers	QF026	Black	size 14	@ £49 each	245.00
3 x Boot-strap trousers	QF027	Black	size 16	@ £54 each	162.00

NET VALUE	897.00
LESS DISCOUNT @ 2.5%	22.42
PLUS CARRIAGE	15.50
SUB TOTAL	890.08
VAT @ 20%	178.02
INVOICE TOTAL £	1,068.10

Terms: 30 days net

Registered in England: 4961029   VAT Registration No: 654 3219 87
Directors: David Cook, Sophie Grainger, Timothy Saunders

Figure 8.3 Example invoice

CREDIT NOTE

The printing and layout of a credit note are similar to an invoice. Sometimes, if an order has not been totally fulfilled, the goods are unsatisfactory or a client has overpaid for some reason, you have to issue a credit note, stating the amount and the reason. Try to relate the credit note to your order number or invoice number – and remember to allow the customer the credit due on the next invoice or statement.

STATEMENT

Quantock Fashions Plc

Taunton Road Bridgwater Somerset TA7 5DQ

Telephone: 01278 687422 Email: quantockfashions@aol.com www.quantockfashions.co.uk

S T A T E M E N T

Statement date: (Today's date)

To: Affordable Fashion
21 Upper High Street
Andover
Hampshire
SP10 4ZU

Invoice date	Invoice number	Net value £	VAT £	Balance due £
(Date of Invoice)	48762	890.08	178.02	1,068.10

Registered in England: 4961029   VAT Registration No: 654 3219 87
Directors: David Cook, Sophie Grainger, Timothy Saunders

Figure 8.4 Example statement

A printed or computer form is desirable, but it can be done on headed paper. Occasionally you have to render a statement of a customer's account – it is often a reminder to pay. Some companies make it a policy to pay only on receipt of a statement. If, through experience, you find out that a company adopts this policy, you should render the statement almost simultaneously with the invoice. Some companies render a document which they call an invoice/statement, and some send out statements of account automatically every month.

The statement should show the dates and numbers of outstanding invoices and details of totals without and with VAT. Details of the products or services need not be included – you have already given this information on the invoices. Some statements include the length of time the invoices have been outstanding, and any payments received during the statement period. Remember to date the statement.

REMITTANCE ADVICE

This should probably be printed, attached to an invoice or statement. When your customers pay you, it is useful for you if they fill in your own remittance advice (some companies make this a tear-off slip on the invoice or statement). Rather like the order, it gives you details which make the book-keeping easier at your end – the details on the remittance advice will be of your choosing, and may include the name, address and customer reference number, your customer's name and address, invoice number, date and totals without and with VAT.

Try it now: Which documents do you need?

Decide which documents you will need for your business, design them and make sure they are ready to use.

The secret of all these documents is to have as few variables on each as possible – all you should have to do when sending the document out is to fill in details relevant to that particular customer. You should not have to fill in document name, your own company name and details, for instance, every time. Use a computer, or get the documents printed.

Your office is the backbone of all your administrative procedures. It should be run efficiently so you do not worry about it, and can get on with the more exciting aspects of your new business – such as selling.

Focus points

✳ Every business will have to do its paperwork, preferably efficiently.

✳ This chapter has given advice on how best to set up your office, considering furniture, equipment, stationery, business documents and, naturally, HASAWA.

✳ Office administration it is yet another aspect of starting a small business, but once it is up and running well you can concentrate on selling your product or service.

Next step

Chapter 9 deals with 'Employing others', so if you are a sole trader, most of it will not apply to you. However, there are some things to think about if you work with contractors or visitors under HASAWA, so it could be worth studying that section. If you are employing others, even if it is only one part-time assistant, you will need to know all the aspects covered in Chapter 9.

Employing others

In this chapter you will learn:

▶ *How to recruit staff, including drawing up a person specification and conducting interviews*

▶ *About the legal rights of employees and the legal responsibilities of employers*

▶ *About the dismissal process*

▶ *About the provisions of the Health and Safety at Work etc. Act 1974 and the Data Protection Act 1998*

▶ *How to manage staff training.*

It is quite a big step to start employing other people when you have been running a business on your own or in partnership. Employing others is not nearly such as minefield as many fear, however. For one thing, it is not true to say that you cannot get rid of an employee who turns out to be totally unreliable or incompetent – you can.

If you set out to be a reasonable, fair and sensible employer, and follow the basic rules about employing others, you have nothing to fear. There are plenty of sources of advice on the law and your statutory obligations: these will be mentioned in this chapter.

Note: The rules and basics on employment law are given as they stand at the time of preparation of this chapter.

Self-assessment: What do you know about employment law?

1 What is the difference between a job description and a schedule of duties?

2 What are the grounds of dismissal?

3 Your comments written on application forms or interview notes might have to be shown to a job applicant – which law covers this?

4 What does SSP stand for?

5 What are the four statutory maternity rights?

6 What is the time limit for issuing an employee with Particulars of Employment?

7 What must you record in your 'accident book'?

8 An employee is entitled to paid holiday. For how many weeks?

9 As an employer, are you obliged to carry out a regular risk assessment?

10 Which government department(s) can give you sound advice on employing others?

Recruitment

The first person you employ is often a friend or a member of the family. How do you go about finding someone you do not know, and selecting the right person to suit you and your methods of working?

PREPARATION

To make sure you get the right person for the job, you must know what you are looking for. It is advisable to draw up a **schedule of duties**, which outlines the job, and a **person specification**, which gives you a profile of the person you are looking for: those elements which are *essential* in the person you want to employ, and those which are *desirable*.

A **job description** is a full description of what the job entails, whom the person is responsible to and any staff they may be required to supervise or manage. If you have been employed, you have probably had a job description or two yourself. As the owner of a small business, a schedule of duties will probably be enough, certainly at this stage. A schedule of duties could look like this:

SCHEDULE OF DUTIES

Job title: WP Operator/clerk

1 Deal with all incoming and outgoing mail and email.

2 Answer the telephone.

3 Write letters and emails.

4 Do the company's book-keeping.

5 Pay wages.

6 Undertake banking.

7 Use the desktop or laptop.

8 Any other job needed to keep the office running smoothly.

Putting 'Any other job' can sound vague, but it does mean that your employee, if they accept the job based on the schedule of duties, agrees to be flexible.

A person specification could look something like this:

PERSON SPECIFICATION Job title: WP Operator/clerk		
	Essential	Desirable
Qualifications:	• GCSE Maths/English or equivalent • Good with figures • WP qualification • Good telephone technique	• NVQ Administration Level 2 • Experience of book-keeping
Practicalities:	• Lives nearby	• Driving licence
Personal qualities:	• Can work without supervision • Flexible	

ADVERTISING

When advertising in the local press or the Job Centre, remember to include in the advertisement at least: job title and brief outline; location; pay; full- or part-time; any special skills, knowledge, experience and personal qualities required; how to apply; closing date.

Your advertisement must not discriminate on grounds of race, sex, disability, age or whether a person is married, single, gay and so on. It is illegal to employ children under 13; children between 13 and school leaving age may be employed under certain conditions; they can be employed to do a paper round, for example. There is no upper age limit for employment, and, with the abolition of the earnings rule, pensioners may now earn as much as they wish. Mature people often make very good employees, especially on a part-time basis.

Remember all you learned about advertisements in Chapter 3 when you were thinking about advertising matter, and make sure any advert you place in the local paper is well displayed, not tucked away in the bottom left-hand corner of an even-numbered page.

SELECTION AND INTERVIEWING

If you are looking for someone to run a small office, and think that 'good with figures' and 'good telephone technique' are essential, you should have some way of testing this. As far as telephone techniques are concerned, you could get applicants to telephone for an application form and make notes of how they deal with you on the phone. 'Good with figures' sometimes requires a simple maths test – GCSE level Maths is not always a sufficient indicator. GCSE level English does not mean that someone is capable of writing good, clear, business English emails or letters.

You can learn quite a lot from the way people fill in an application form, so try to use one. The areas normally covered in an application for employment form are: name; address; skills; qualifications; employment history; outside interests. Send the schedule of duties out with the application form.

Try it now: Recruitment checklist

Presuming you have decided to employ another or others, there are several steps to be taken. This checklist will help ensure that you have done everything:

* Write person specification. ☐
* Write schedule of duties. ☐
* Decide hours required. ☐
* Decide pay. ☐
* Design advert. ☐
* Place advert. ☐
* Sift replies. ☐
* Write to rejects. ☐
* Schedule interviews. ☐
* Make interview notes. ☐
* Write to chosen applicant. ☐
* Write to rejects. ☐

Ask the applicants to complete the form in their own handwriting if possible, so you can see whether they can write neatly, can spell correctly and so on, if this is important to the job. Probably many, if not most, job applications will be made online. The previous work experience can also be very revealing: it can give you a good idea of whether a prospective employee can hold down a job for a sensible length of time, or whether he or she tends to flit from job to job. Explore any gaps (even of a few months) in the working history. It could be that the applicant has been in prison. This is not a necessarily good reason for rejecting an applicant out of hand, but you need to know.

Look out for any discrepancies in the way the form has been completed. If people are less than truthful on an application form, they might be slightly less than honest in their employment. If you ask for 'hobbies' on the form, explore what applicants mean by their replies. For example, 'football': does this mean they play (in which case they are probably fit) or do they watch? For 'music', if they listen, that is different from playing an instrument, which requires perseverance and manipulative skills. If they play in a group, band or orchestra, it shows you they are used to working withothers.

From the application forms, select perhaps three or four to interview. Reject at once any which do not fulfil the essential requirements, and reply to all those who apply, even if it is only to say 'no'.

When you interview applicants, ask questions to get them talking about themselves and what they can offer you and why they want the job. Asking open questions – 'What did you do?' 'Why did you…?' 'How did you…?' – helps to get them talking about their skills, knowledge, experience and personality. Of course, you should also make sure they understand not only what the terms and conditions of employment are, but also what the job entails.

Discuss the schedule of duties at the interview stage; it will give you an opportunity to find out where any weaknesses lie and where training would be needed. Be aware that under the Data Protection Act comments written on application forms or interview notes could have to be shown to the applicant. They could also be used in evidence by an unsuccessful applicant who claims their failure to get the job was because of discrimination on the grounds of sex, race, age, sexual orientation, religion or belief and disability.

Use the interview fully so that each side can find out as much as possible about each other. It takes time, but it is time well invested. A good employee will stay with you and quickly become part of the company. Employees who do not fit in leave, and then you have to start all over again.

Once you have made your selection, make a formal job offer in writing to the successful applicant, and once you have had a definite acceptance in writing, write to those who were not successful.

Pay and benefits

Calculating pay, benefits and deductions is fairly complicated. It can be done manually, but is much better done on computer, which, if fed the right information, will do all the calculations and print out the payslips, P45s and P60s.

The amount of gross pay, plus overtime rates if applicable, will have been agreed between you at the interview/job offer stage. It is also useful to agree at that early stage:

▶ the **method** of payment – straight into bank account or building society by credit transfer, cheque or cash

▶ the **frequency** of payment – weekly or monthly.

From an employer's point of view it is much less of a security risk to pay straight into an account by credit transfer. It is also more economical to pay monthly rather than weekly, because you usually pay in arrears, so you have the use of that money for about three weeks. An employee might wish to be paid weekly in cash. You, as the employer, must make up your mind what you are prepared to do and stick to it. You can ask an employee to change once he or she has started work, but it is better to lay down conditions of employment at the start.

As an employer you are committed to pay the employee the amounts and on the terms agreed, which must not be below the national minimum hourly rate (see the BIS website: www.bis.gov. uk). BIS stands for the Department for Business Innovation and Skills. You must pay this, no matter what state the business is in.

You also have to make statutory deductions from the gross pay. These are:

- income tax

- National Insurance – employee's contribution. The employer's contribution is paid over and above the agreed wage of the employee, and is a percentage of that figure.

For all details of deductions, how they should be collected and how and when paid to the authorities, tax tables and so on, ask the DWP and HM Revenue & Customs. ACAS also do a very helpful leaflet called 'Employing people: a handbook for small firms'. You can download this from the ACAS website (www. acas.org.uk) or pick up a copy from the Job Centre.

You must supply the employee with the following:

- **Detailed wage/salary slip** showing the gross pay, all deductions and the net amount payable. It does not matter if the slip is handwritten, but it must be given with the pay.

- An **annual P60** showing the amount of tax deducted in that financial year. This is the government's financial year from 5 April to 4 April, not the company's financial year.

- If the employee leaves your employment, a **P45** showing the amount of tax deducted to date in that financial year. Your accountant can advise on this.

STATUTORY SICK PAY (SSP)

As an employer, if your employee falls sick and is away for up to three working days, you do not have to pay them, but if he or she is off sick for four or more days, you must pay the employee sick pay, instead of a wage, for up to 28 weeks. You can get a rebate from the government if you keep details of people off sick; otherwise you have to pay for this. There are strict rules about how much must be paid, when and to whom, and about doctors' certificates. Ask your local DWP for details and help if you are having to do this for the first time, and keep records. Other than SSP there is no legal requirement to pay employees who are off sick.

MATERNITY RIGHTS AND PAY

A pregnant woman has four statutory rights:

1 **Time off with pay for antenatal care:** she does not need to have worked for you for a specific length of time.

2 **Statutory Maternity Pay** if she has worked for you for at least 26 weeks up to the fifteenth week before the expected week of confinement (EWC). You can claim this back.

3 The right to **52 weeks' maternity leave** with maintenance of all benefits except pay. The leave can start from 11 weeks before the birth and be up to 52 weeks in total.

4 The right to **return to work** after maternity leave if she wishes.

There are detailed rules about managing maternity leave and pay and returning to work. Ask the DWP (www.dwp.gov.uk) for details on all these points.

PARENTAL LEAVE

Both parents of a baby have the right to 13 weeks' unpaid leave to be taken before the child's fifth birthday – or eighteenth birthday if the child is disabled. New fathers who have been employed with you for over 26 weeks are entitled to two weeks' leave paid at the minimum statutory rate. This can be recovered from the Department of Work and Pensions (www.dwp.gov. uk). For information on paternity rights, visit www.gov.uk and follow the links.

PENSIONS

Starting from October 2012, you must enrol employees aged 22 and over into a workplace pension (also called an occupational pension) if you don't already operate such a scheme. For more information, go to www.gov.uk and follow the links to the pensions section.

HOLIDAY

All full-time employees are entitled to 28 days' annual paid holiday, which includes bank and public holidays. Part-time workers accrue their entitlement pro rata. For details on how the minimum holiday rules operate, see the booklet 'A Guide to Working Time Regulations', which you can download from www.hse.gov.uk, or check out www.bis.gov.uk or www.businesslink.gov.uk

> **Remember this:** Keep to your agreement
>
> You *must* pay your employees the agreed amount and on the terms agreed. You have no wriggle room on this.

Particulars of Employment

An employer is obliged, within two months of an employee starting the job, to give an employee written Particulars of Employment. There should be two copies of the document, signed by both parties – one copy to each.

This statement must be set out in one single document and include the following:

1 Names of employer and employee

2 Start date of employment

3 Rate of pay, how it is calculated and when it will be paid

4 Hours of work, including normal working hours

5 Holiday entitlement

6 The employee's job title – or brief description of work

7 Place of work

8 Pension arrangements

9 Sick pay arrangements, if any

10 End date of employment – for short-term contracts

11 Period of notice

12 Grievance and disciplinary procedures

13 Particulars of collective agreements which directly affect the employee's terms and conditions

See the ACAS website for details of their helpful booklets on contracts, handbooks and procedures: www.acas.org.uk

DISMISSAL

You can dismiss people for:

▶ lack of capability, which covers poor performance and inability to do the job because of a medical condition/absence

▶ misconduct

▶ redundancy

▶ drug or alcohol abuse

▶ special circumstances (e.g. loss of driving licence if driving licence is essential to the job)

▶ any other substantial business reason.

You can dismiss people who have up to one year's service with the company without a reason. If you have dismissed a pregnant woman or someone with over one year's service, you are required to give one of the above reasons, in writing, for the dismissal. You can no longer dismiss someone because of their age; the default retirement age has been abolished.

In nearly all circumstances it is essential to follow a disciplinary procedure before dismissing an employee:

1 verbal warning – noted in book

2 written warning

3 final written warning.

Instant dismissal for a grave offence, such as proven theft, is legal. The point of the legislation is to ensure that people are not dismissed out of hand for no good reason without a fair hearing. An employer must:

▶ Give a written note of the issues

▶ Allow a fair and unbiased hearing

▶ Listen to mitigation

- Allow the employee to be accompanied by a colleague or accredited trade union official

- Give the right of appeal, even if the appeal is to the person who took the decision in the first place.

Provided you deal with your employees reasonably, and with understanding, you should not fall foul of the law. It is worth documenting all that happens very carefully, in case you have to answer to an employment tribunal. Again ACAS publishes helpful booklets on this. An unfairly dismissed employee may be reinstated or awarded compensation to be paid by the employer.

PERIOD OF NOTICE

These are the *minimum* periods of notice an employer must give to an employee:

- Up to one month's service – none

- Between one month's and two years' service – one week

- After two years – one week's notice for each complete year of service until (s)he has more than 12 years' service, when the minimum period remains at 12 weeks.

An employee can leave without notice during the first month of service. After that an employee has an obligation to give at least a week's notice. Longer periods for both parties are normally written into the Particulars of Employment. Notice must be paid, even if you ask the person to leave before the end of the notice period.

You can only make an employee retire if you notified them before 6 April 2011 and they were over 65 before 1 October 2011. In this case you must give them at least six months' notice of the date of their retirement. They have a right to ask to continue working after normal retirement age – which should not be less than 65 years. Refer to the BIS website for details (www.bis.gov.uk).

REDUNDANCY

It is unlikely that you will get into a redundancy situation in the early years of the business. Redundancy occurs if, for some reason, the job no longer exists, and therefore you have to end someone's employment.

There are rules about redundancy and redundancy payments which you can obtain from the BIS.

WORKING HOURS

The Working Time Regulations 1998 impose rules on total weekly working hours, limits on night work, health assessments, rest periods, breaks and annual holiday. See the HSE booklet and website for helpful examples and guidance.

FLEXIBLE WORKING

Any employee can request a flexible working arrangement, and more and more organizations are extending the offer to all or part of their workforce. Some employees have a statutory right to ask (for example if they have a child under 17) and in these cases you have to have good business reasons for rejecting the request.

DISCRIMINATION

You must make sure you have equal pay and benefits for equal work – pro-rated for part-timers. You must not discriminate on grounds of sex, race, age, sexual orientation, religion or belief and disability in any aspect of employment; and any harassment on those grounds can also be found to be discriminatory by an employment tribunal.

Remember this: Create an employees' booklet

It is useful to create a small booklet with all this information listed, with blanks for filling in a particular employee's details.

HASAWA and Data Protection Act

HASAWA

As an employer, you have a common duty of care towards your employees. The Health and Safety at Work etc. Act 1974 and a range of health and safety regulations require all employers, self-employed people and employees not to put themselves or anyone else – including contractors or visitors, for instance – at risk.

Employers have an additional responsibility to ensure that the working environment – including offices – will not be detrimental to the safety and health of employees, contractors and anyone else working on their premises. This includes safe systems, storage, materials and machinery, as well as proper fire precautions, access and procedures.

Case study: Assessing potential risks

Some years ago a young factory employee had a serious accident when cleaning a particular machine. The employer had ignored, or forgotten, the regulations for that machine which ruled that a young employee under the age of 18 could operate the machine, but not clean it, which involved taking the machine apart and exposing sharp cutting surfaces.

You should assess all potential risks in your workplace. For example, if you were a wood turner employing an apprentice, your risk assessment could be set out like this and would cover:

Risk	Assessment dates	Training completed dates
Use of machinery (each machine detailed)		
Machinery guards		
Cleaning machines		
Use of tools		
Storage of tools		
Storage of materials		
Protective clothing		
Lifting and handling techniques		
Fire extinguishers: maintenance and use		
Sufficient lighting		
Heating		
Ventilation		
Accident book		

When carrying out the risk assessment, the following areas are the main ones to consider; a wood turner might have other risks, such as access to premises.

▶ **Machinery**

   ▷ For each machine the wood turner would note its condition, its safeguards, its safe use and its cleaning routines.

▶ **Protective clothing**

   ▷ What should be supplied and worn?

▶ **Lifting and handling techniques**

   ▷ There are safe ways to lift and handle materials or move machines.

▶ **Fire precautions**

   ▷ Smoking is prohibited in enclosed workplaces, but are other fire precautions and appliances in place?

▷ Are fire extinguishers kept topped up and does everyone know how to use them?

▷ Are all fire exits kept clear?

▶ **Heating, lighting and ventilation**

▷ Is there enough light to see and work safely?

▷ Is the workplace warm enough to keep hands flexible?

▷ Is there enough ventilation?

It is up to the wood turner to make sure all the necessary procedures are in place and to train the apprentice and monitor his or her safe working, but it is also up to the apprentice to work safely and not endanger himself or herself and anyone else, including suppliers, visitors and customers.

Take reasonable precautionary measures, train people regularly in the procedures and monitor any changes. There are additional obligations to protect new or expectant mothers, including a specific assessment. Businesses dealing with food of any sort also have food hygiene regulations to comply with.

Your workplace should be clean, and properly ventilated, lit and heated. Other businesses will have different risks: the risks of working in an office, including trip hazards and safe storage were covered in Chapter 8. All other employers, however small their workforce, have a duty to ensure the health and safety of their staff and should carry out a risk assessment.

▶ **Policy statement**

If you employ five people or more, you are obliged to draw up a Health and Safety Policy Statement, and display it where every employee can read it. If you have more than 20 employees, you have to have a Fire Certificate.

▶ **Accident book**

You are also obliged to keep a record of all accidents – normally in an accident book. An entry in the accident book must show:

- name, sex, age, occupation of victim
- nature of injury and place where it occurred
- description of circumstances.

For full details of regulations, see HSE booklets.

▶ First aid

Higher-risk workplaces must have a qualified first-aider on the premises. For lower-risk workplaces you do not need a first-aider until you have 50 employees, and for medium-risk workplaces 20 employees. However, it is sensible, if possible, to have someone who can administer first aid.

At the very least, you should have a first-aid box, easily accessible and regularly topped up. For details of what the box should contain, plus a full clear description of what to do, see the *First Aid Manual* published jointly by the British Red Cross Society, St John Ambulance Brigade and St Andrew's Ambulance Association, obtainable from bookshops. Check whether you are permitted to dispense medication of any sort.

DATA PROTECTION ACT

Our personal data is stored and used by all sorts of companies and organizations. Insurance companies know exactly when your car insurance is due for renewal – even though you are not with them – and may bombard you with junk mail. Government departments, local government, health authorities and credit card agencies know a great deal about you. So do retail outlets with in-store credit cards and systems which analyse what sort of shopper you are. However, we do have certain rights to protect our personal data under the Data Protection Act 1998 and you, as an employer of others, have a duty to protect your employees' personal data.

This act applies to data held electronically – on computer, even if it is only a laptop – and manual data such as handwritten or typed records which are held in a filing system.

If you have processed any personal data about your employees beyond just names and addresses – for instance, if you have personal information about rates of pay, domestic circumstances and so on, you must register with the Information Commissioner but be wary of bogus registration agencies.

Your employees have a right to know what personal data is being held, and whether it is correct. In practice, this means that most employers give their employees a printout of the information held once a year, and ask them to confirm or update it.

If you are using personal data purely for personnel reasons with your company, you are unlikely to have problems. Problems arise when you use or disclose that data for some other purpose – selling employee lists to a marketing company, for example.

Here again, provided employers go about their business in a normal, straightforward and fair way, they should not fall foul of the law. For further details see the Information Commissioner's Office website – www.ico.gov.uk

Try it now: 'Employing others' quiz

Are these statements true or false?

1 A person specification should list 'essential' and 'desirable'.
2 A schedule of duties and a job description are the same thing.
3 A rejected job applicant has no right to see interview notes.
4 It is illegal to employ children aged under 13.
5 There is an upper age limit for employment.
6 It is illegal to discriminate on the grounds of sex, race, sexual orientation or disability only.
7 An employer must deduct income tax from an employee's pay.
8 An employer must provide a detailed wage or salary slip.
9 An employer must pay Statutory Sick Pay to an employee who is off sick.
10 An employer can claim back Statutory Maternity Pay.
11 New fathers are entitled to two weeks' paid leave.
12 An employer need not operate an occupational pension scheme.
13 All employees are entitled to 28 days' paid holiday per year.
14 An employer must provide written Particulars of Employment.
15 An employer may not dismiss an employee for incompetence.
16 All employees are entitled to at least one week's notice to leave.
17 Self-employed people have no obligations under HASAWA.
18 Employees have a right to know what personal data is being held.

(The answers can be found at the end of this book.)

Staff training

If you have been employed, you will almost certainly have been on training courses of various sorts, and have received on-the-job training, which may have been carried out in a formal or an informal manner. If you are now employing other people, it is part of your job to make sure your staff receive appropriate training.

Staff training is not necessarily about sending people away on courses, although this might be required sometimes. Staff training is about making people efficient and productive and enabling them to enjoy doing their work because they do it well. Most staff training can be done at the place of work.

Well-trained staff are much more likely to give good customer service than staff who are left to work things out for themselves; staff who are knowledgeable about the products, the company procedures (including the complaints procedure) and how to deal with customers and clients will feel confident in their own abilities.

INDUCTION TRAINING

New staff, or at least new to you, need good induction training, even if they are experienced in the skills of their job. Induction training should cover all a new employee needs to know fairly quickly, although not necessarily all on the first day. It should cover:

► whereabouts of facilities (toilet, kettle, etc.)

► security of personal possessions

► break times and what people normally do

► fire precautions and procedures

- introduction to colleagues
- whereabouts of materials, equipment, etc. needed for the job
- basic job procedures
- basic company rules, regulations and customs
- someone to turn to.

It is time-consuming to train new people, but it is better than leaving them to dive in at the deep end.

DEVELOPMENT TRAINING

People need training and retraining all their working lives as laws, systems, machinery and equipment change. It is helpful to make a simple training plan for yourself and each member of your team to make sure you are all up to Experienced Worker Standard (EWS) on all aspects of your business. Not everyone will need to know everything, although in a small business most of the team need to know most things. Sam, for example, who perhaps has one new part-time assistant in her Affordable Fashion boutique, could make a training plan like this:

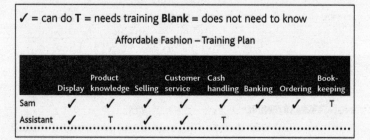

✓ = can do **T** = needs training **Blank** = does not need to know

Affordable Fashion – Training Plan

	Display	Product knowledge	Selling	Customer service	Cash handling	Banking	Ordering	Book-keeping
Sam	✓	✓	✓	✓	✓	✓	✓	T
Assistant	✓	T	✓	✓	T			

It is a very simple plan and quick to do, but it clarifies what training needs to be done. It is the training itself which takes a bit of time.

Try it now: Create a training plan

Make a training plan for your own team, including yourself, covering the various tasks needed for each of you to perform efficiently and productively.

Case study: Training

Following Sam's training plan, she needs to train her new assistant in cash handling procedures, breaking that task down into manageable chunks. Each till is a little different so a new assistant will need to know the vagaries of this one. Take 'ringing up' the items as an example:

Explain

Sam would tell the assistant exactly how to ring up the price for each garment and why it is important to press the right keys to get a breakdown of sales. Sam needs to know which items sell better than others, even when she is not in the shop.

Demonstrate

Sam would show the assistant exactly how to ring up a variety of items, preferably privately when no customers are present. This is the point at which people often think they have done the training – they have told and shown, and then leave the 'trainee' to it. The next two steps are just as important.

Try out

Sam would let her new assistant try out the procedure while Sam watches.

Correct

This way, Sam can, if necessary, correct any mistakes the assistant makes, then and there.

When Sam and her assistant are both satisfied they know what they are doing, the assistant can do the task for real, with Sam keeping an eye open and being there for support if the assistant needs help.

Ringing up is a simple task, easily learned, but needs to be done correctly. Other, more complicated, tasks will take longer to learn, but if the sequence is followed, the learning will be that much quicker and more efficient.

▶ The training sequence

For on-the-job training in general, follow this sequence:

1 **Explain:** Tell the learner not only what is to be done, but why and how it fits in to other jobs.

2 **Demonstrate:** Show the learner how to do the job – slowly.

3 **Try out:** Let the learner do the job while you are still there to watch.

4 **Correct:** Put right any mistakes early on – bad habits are difficult to correct later. This is particularly important where safety is concerned.

Focus points

✷ This chapter has pointed you in helpful directions to make sure you comply with all the employment legislation. It has not gone into detail on every point because legislation changes so frequently.

✷ You must ensure you do not break the law when considering recruitment, pay and conditions, your employee's rights and HASAWA, so consult the websites mentioned for the most up-to-date information.

✷ Employing others can be daunting, but in many cases you cannot manage on your own. If you are a sensible, fair employer and have good systems and procedures to work with, you should not have many problems.

Next step

If you are opening a shop, the next chapter is full of advice, hints and tips on all the things you need to think about. If not, skip to Chapter 11 about 'Running a home and a business', a delicate balancing act for all self-employed people.

Opening a shop

In this chapter you will learn:

▶ *About siting your shop – will it be on a prime site alongside the high-street chains or on a secondary site away from the main shopping district?*

▶ *How to develop the right image for your shop, including the décor and staff*

▶ *How and when to carry out stocktaking*

▶ *How to put in place the range of security measures required for a shop*

▶ *How to market your shop, especially during the run-up to opening day.*

People who open a shop usually have some retail experience or work with a partner who does. Retailing is a way of life. It can be very rewarding, but it is hard work and not for the fainthearted.

Self-assessment: Considerations when opening a shop

1 What is your customer profile?

2 Who will be your suppliers?

3 Where is your shop to be sited?

4 What image do you want to portray?

5 Who will work with you?

6 How much start-up capital will you need?

7 What are the legal requirements?

8 How will you keep your stock at the right level and secure?

9 What will be your marketing strategy?

10 Are you excited at the prospect of opening a shop?

You may not be able to answer all these questions now, but you should be able to answer questions 1 and 2 from your work with Chapter 1. You should be able to answer 'yes' to question 10.

Siting

RIGHT FOR THE MARKET

In deciding where your outlet should be sited, it is useful to ask yourself whether what you are offering is largely something which customers will buy on impulse if they happen to see it, or whether it is something they need, so will seek you out, within reason, wherever you happen to be.

This means you have two broad categories from which to choose – prime sites and secondary sites.

▶ **Prime sites**

A prime site is where you will find the 'big boys', the household names which customers expect to find in any worthwhile shopping venue.

Prime sites are expensive, and a question you need to ask yourself is: 'If I choose a unit in a prime site, will people passing my door on their way to the branches of the national multiples be tempted to stop and consider my wares – and will they do it in sufficient numbers to justify the expense?'

▶ Secondary sites

Secondary sites are located away from the prime site areas. Naturally, the outgoings on a secondary site are lower than those for a prime site. The level of trade could well be lower, too, so you will probably need to tell the public that you are there, which means that advertising costs for a secondary site could be greater than those for a prime site. Many small shops site themselves on the periphery of a small town.

POSITION

Whether prime or secondary, it is worth considering the position of your outlet. For example, would you want to be actually fronting the street with pedestrians and traffic passing by or would you prefer to be within a shopping centre?

In considering a site it might be worth seeing who your neighbours will be. What type of goods will they be offering? Will they be in direct competition with you? Will they attract people who might equally be interested in what you have to offer?

SIZE AND SHAPE

Two units with the same square footage could offer good or bad possibilities depending on the shape and the type of stock to be fitted into it. So before tramping off to the agents or around the town centres, consider:

- ▶ the optimum size of the unit you need (do not forget stockroom and office space as well)

- ▶ the most appropriate shape for the type of business you are intending to run.

For example, a deep, narrow shop with very little frontage would be acceptable for a counter service operation – like a jeweller's or a motor accessories shop – but would be unsuitable for a self-service shop – like a mini-market – where customers need more space to walk around selecting their own items.

PUBLIC TRANSPORT AND PARKING

Customers need to be able to get to and from your shop easily and conveniently, whether by public transport or under their own steam. When deciding on the siting of your potential outlet, ease of access for customers is something else to consider.

ACCESS FOR DELIVERIES

As well as thinking about how convenient it is for your customers to get to your store, it is as well to take into account how your stock will be delivered to you in the first place.

For any potential site, see what access there is for suppliers' or carriers' vehicles, and how easy it is to transfer items from a vehicle to your goods-in area.

THE COMPETITION

Consider whether it would be to your advantage to open up a shop opposite an existing outlet which sells a similar range of goods to you:

▶ Advantages

▶ Customers can easily make comparisons between outlets offering similar goods.

▶ You can highlight your business with special offers or other features which the competition is not doing.

▶ Disadvantages

▶ Customers continue to support the existing outlet through force of habit.

▶ Competitors can anticipate your opening, and mount their own campaigns to distract attention from you in those critical early days.

You might then think it wise to set up among outlets which offer goods different from those you are planning to sell, so that you are, in effect, the sole supplier in that particular locality.

> ### Try it now: Pretend you are a customer
> Try to park and find out where the buses stop, then walk to your proposed shop, stop and examine the outside of your shop and that of your potential neighbours. Go round the back, if you can, to see whether customers could pick up their purchases at the back door, particularly if you sell large items.

Image

Your image must, naturally, depend on what you are selling, who your customers are likely to be and where your shop is sited. But it will also depend on your fixtures and fittings, décor and lighting, opening hours and the people who work in your shop.

FIXTURES AND FITTINGS

The way your stock is presented to customers will depend a great deal on the type of fixtures you are using. If you are taking over a unit, you might well feel that you can make do with the fixtures left by the previous occupier. If yours is quite a different type of business, though, it might not be a wise decision if it means your stock is not shown off to the best advantage. Perhaps a slight adaptation will do the trick, but it could be a false economy if you are not doing justice to your stock.

DÉCOR AND LIGHTING

Outward appearances are important to a retail outlet. Look at the various styles of decoration used by businesses, as well as the variety of colour schemes, and try to decide what would be the most suitable decoration for the outside of your premises.

Having made the premises look attractive and inviting from the outside, you must continue that appeal into the interior. Do your research again, and see what other people do, particularly in your line of business.

A very important aspect of your internal decorations is the lighting. This really is an area which needs to be considered carefully: consider level of lighting, type of lighting (fluorescent, spot, and so on), direction of lighting and use of natural light.

OPENING HOURS

The trend is for retail outlets to be open for six-day trading and in some businesses for seven. This arrangement might not be quite so easy for you if you are working on your own. Alternatively you might close for half a day according to local custom, or as dictated by local bye-laws. If your unit is situated within a shopping centre, your opening hours will be governed by the rules of the establishment.

Whatever the situation, you must make sure that your opening hours enhance your image rather than detract from it. Your image must be that you are there and open for business when customers want to spend their money.

Consider your opening hours carefully. If you state on your shop window (and you must put an 'opening hours' notice in the window or door) that you open at 9.00 a.m., then you *must* open at 9.00. If you don't, customers will go elsewhere.

PEOPLE

People form an important part of a retail outlet. How many people you will need in your shop will relate to your pattern of trading. You will need to consider whether to use all full-time staff, or perhaps supplement these with part-timers for peak trading times.

You will need to decide how your staff will be dressed; whether they will be provided with a uniform, or whether ordinary everyday clothes will be suitable – is suitable formal or casual? What will *you* be wearing?

The hours of work will relate both to trade and financial considerations. Remember that there is more to paying staff than just wages; for instance, you are responsible for National Insurance contributions. See Chapter 9 for detailed information.

Suitable conditions of employment for members of staff will include the type of facilities you will need to provide, such as toilet and washing facilities, a cloakroom locker, providing suitable security for personal belongings, and refreshment facilities, even if it is only for making tea or coffee.

> **Remember this: Fashion retailing requires fashionable staff**
>
> If you happen to sell jewellery, clothing or other fashion items, make sure you and your staff wear something which goes along with that image. But remember that you'll be on your feet all day, so don't go overboard on the shoes.

Stock, suppliers and stocktaking

STOCK

Stock is money, and stock on the shelves is money waiting to be transferred to the cash register drawer.

You will need a carefully considered range of stock, sufficient to offer customers a suitable choice. Getting the balance right is the key; there must not be so much as to be confusing, nor yet too little for the choice to be unreasonably restricted.

So, do you try and go for the image of:

▶ having whatever customers are likely to want?

▶ satisfying the majority, leaving the minority customers to seek satisfaction elsewhere?

▶ specializing, and catering for the minority?

SUPPLIERS

You will have considered your suppliers in Chapter 1. Carry this information forward and hone your ideas to make sure, as far as you can, that you will be well supplied with the right stock, particularly if you are importing stock.

What you are looking for in a supplier is a reliable service, a continuity of supply and an acceptable range of lines. Unless you can get these, your image is going to suffer with your customers when they keep finding you are out of stock of the lines they want to buy, particularly the popular ones.

When sourcing suppliers take these points into account:

▶ Visit trade fairs and the Internet.

▶ Find out who your competitors are using.

▶ Will you deal direct or through agents?

▶ Take heed of recommendations by (friendly) competitors.

▶ Take trips abroad and visit UK suppliers.

▶ Be aware that some suppliers require minimum orders.

▶ Some suppliers may require the first payment up front because you have little or no trading history.

▶ Factor in the carriage costs.

Try it now: List your required suppliers

If you have not already done so, it is most important that you do this now. Make a list of all the suppliers you will need and draw up a chart. Use Sam's Affordable Fashion suppliers chart in Chapter 1 as an example.

STOCKTAKING

Good, computerized, stock and order systems are a great asset. Your stock level is automatically adjusted every time you sell an item. However, this doesn't account for stolen or damaged items, so a physical stocktake is still necessary.

Stocktaking is an exercise to establish a current record of stock in hand at any given time. This is necessary, not only to establish the number of items, but also the cash value.

Do the stocktaking at least once a year for the inclusion of the stock in the annual accounts. In practice, a full stocktaking could well be done twice yearly or even quarterly. It is possible that in certain sections within a shop stock would need to be taken weekly, or, in the case of very perishable items, daily, to provide the basis for an effective stock and order system.

We are concerned here, though, with the general stocktake. Accuracy is paramount for a stocktaking exercise. It is not a job to be rushed or fitted in between other things; it needs full concentration to get it right. This is why, very likely, you will find yourself doing this job out of trading hours, or at a weekend if the shop is closed.

The overall rule to follow for a successful stocktake is for everything to be methodical – the preparation, the execution and the follow-up.

Case study

A shop in our locality which sells low-priced dresses finds that customers rip the dresses off their security tags to try them on, and then leave the dresses on the floor. How would you account for that in your stocktaking?

Money, security and legal requirements

MONEY

A retail shop, by its very nature, is bound to be involved in money. You will need to consider how best to handle cash, cheques and debit and credit cards at the point of sale including the chip and PIN system. This will require a set procedure to be devised, and it is important that everybody involved keeps to the system. For this to happen it would probably be helpful to have your procedure written down.

Taking money at the cashpoint can be a good opportunity to record those details which can provide useful management information, for example, by dissecting sales into suitable groups either by product, department or section. This will be a simple and effective way of creating data for management control, such as the basis for a stock and order system.

At certain times money will need to be banked. Establish a regular routine for this, but preferably not a regular route to and from the bank premises. We will consider this further in the next section – Security.

The two essential elements for this task are the preparation of moneys for banking, and the recording of banking transactions. The underlying requirement for this is accuracy. Again, you will need a definite procedure for this, which must be followed by all concerned.

SECURITY

Security should be a continual theme in all aspects of business activity. In this section we will consider four important areas: staff, stock, money and premises.

▶ Staff

All members of staff should be security-minded. It is as much in their own interest as it is for the business, always to be alert to situations where security is not all it might be. Encourage staff to come to you about any apparent lapses in security procedures, and with ideas for improving security arrangements – be sure to be receptive when they do. Security is an important subject which concerns every member of staff in some way or another – it helps if they are aware of this.

Unfortunately, staff pilferage can be a major source of loss if not prevented. One very simple precaution: do not allow staff who handle cash to have their handbags or wallets anywhere near the cashpoint. In any case, these valuable items of personal property should be securely locked away.

▶ Stock

The security of stock should be a continuous and conscious process. In the sales area, apart from stock actually on display, remember that security includes accurate ringing up of prices, and being aware of the various dodges which can be used by customers for taking stock items past a cashpoint without paying for them. For example, taking items through in their own bags, hiding items in pockets or under coats, switching low-priced tickets on to high-priced items, not completely clearing a wire basket or trolley, are all methods used by customers to avoid payment.

In the storage area the accurate checking in of deliveries of stock is a very important part of stock security: a business cannot afford to pay suppliers for items of stock it never received.

If your shop is likely to handle highly pilferable items – perhaps lines which are small in size but high in value – then consider the best arrangements you can make for their security, for example, a locked security cage in the security area, and keeping them behind glass or behind the counter in the sales area. Perhaps alarmed wires threaded through stock items in the sales area, as often seen on displays of hi-fi equipment etc., could be effective.

▶ Money

Security and money would seem naturally to go together. Once again, there are various situations to consider, and to decide on set procedures or systems to meet them.

The simple device of making sure the cash register drawer is kept open for the least possible time, and certainly firmly shut between the end of one customer's order and starting the next, is a good security system to adopt.

Where cash is stored, security should be as effective as possible, particularly when cash is actually being handled and stored.

Whatever the situation, you will need some form of safe; take advice on this from your local Crime Prevention Officer. Incidentally, you have to remember floor loadings when considering the installation of a safe – the floor has to be strong enough to hold it. Safe companies will no doubt be pleased to advise you.

We mentioned earlier that we would consider the security aspects of banking. Decide how you are intending to transport moneys to and from your bank. The varying of times and route as far as is reasonable is a simple, but effective method. If it is also possible to vary the personnel involved occasionally, that could be useful.

There are several security firms who will undertake to carry moneys to and from the bank on your behalf. Talk to other businesses and to your bank manager, and try to get as much independent advice as possible about the various security firms who operate in your area before committing yourself; once again a talk with your local Crime Prevention Officer might prove fruitful.

▶ Premises

There is a great variety of devices designed to offer security for premises, ranging from the simple idea of placing convex mirrors at strategic points within the sales or storage areas to allow vision of otherwise blind spots, to complicated networks of video cameras and monitors. The aim is to use a system which is the most appropriate to your needs and the needs of your premises.

Do not overlook the traditional alarm bell, particularly one which can be connected to your local police station. Suitable padlocks can provide adequate security for everyday situations inside and outside the building. Keeping doors open for the least possible time, particularly at goods-in when receiving deliveries, is a sensible security measure.

You can still find shops which have the old-fashioned hanging bell on a spring over the shop door; at least a variation on that theme lets you know that someone has entered the premises if you have been called away from the sales area.

Ask advice of your local Crime Prevention Officer as well as your insurance company on the subject of security of premises. It could save you spending too much money – and losing a great deal of money and stock.

Case study: Security for retailers

At a seminar for retailers, one shopkeeper complained about customers running off with small, pilferable items: the shop sold newspapers, snacks and other small items. Another shopkeeper explained he never had problems with that sort of thing: he sold pianos!

LEGAL REQUIREMENTS

When running a shop you should know the provisions of:

- the Trade Descriptions Act
- the Sale of Goods Act
- the Offices, Shops and Railway Premises Act
- consumer protection legislation
- local bye-laws
- fire prevention requirements
- the Health and Safety at Work etc. Act (HASAWA).

All the legislation is drafted to make sure shopkeepers sell goods which are of 'merchantable quality', properly described and at a price which is fair to the shopkeeper and the consumer.

If you do not know the necessary details of the law relating to keeping a shop, contact the Trading Standards Officer for your local authority.

The Fire and Rescue Service will advise you on what you must do to qualify for a fire certificate for your premises.

You will need to have third-party insurance for your staff and customers – consult an insurance broker who specializes in small shops.

Marketing

Potential customers will need to know that you and your shop are there, so take every opportunity to advertise your business. This need not restrict itself solely to advertising material.

METHODS

For example, if you will be needing staff for your shop, remember that you, yourself, will be advertising your business by your appearance, manner and so forth during interviews with applicants: an excellent opportunity for creating a good business image.

Produce some suitable material – well presented – for applicants to take home: another good and subtle way of getting your name known in these critical early stages. For example, give candidates a small leaflet setting out the basic hours and working conditions, holidays and so on. Make sure the shop's name and logo are prominently displayed on the leaflet. You should also take the trouble to notify unsuccessful applicants – it is worth the price of a few stamps in goodwill.

For your more formal advertising, you will no doubt make use of the local press. Compile a press release feature about you and your business and talk to the advertising manager of the paper about a combined campaign – involving some straight advertising (which you pay for) and an advertising feature (which you get for free) on your business.

A less formal means of advertising, but one which could be effective for advertising the location of your premises, is a door-to-door leaflet distribution within your catchment area. Some local papers will undertake this task for you – it could be worth raising the matter when talking about advertising matters generally. Have a look at Chapter 4 to remind yourself of things to think about when producing an advertising leaflet.

Do not overlook the opportunity which the shop premises themselves provide for advertising. The actual shop front will present an image to the passing public. Suitable posters on the windows will carry particular messages, even if it is only to advertise the day of opening of your new enterprise.

TIMING

Having considered what advertising methods to use, you should also think about when to use them. Timing is significant, particularly when advertising something new, like the opening of a new shop.

Your 'Coming shortly' or 'Opening soon' advertising which could be appearing in the local press should be timed to arouse initial interest (the AIDA formula, see Chapter 4), followed by a second wave of advertising to carry on the momentum up to the moment of opening with, perhaps, a final reminder to say 'We are now here'.

As well as the general press advertising, you might consider a leaflet distribution related specifically to the day of opening, combined with a special offer valid only for opening day.

OPENING DAY

When the great day arrives, make sure you try to get the most out of it. The use of large posters on the shop windows announcing the fact is probably a good start.

Are you considering having someone special to declare the premises open? If so, will the public come to see that person and buy things from your shop? Remember the value of the press release and of press coverage; make sure a photographer is ready to hand.

Maybe a special offer – a voucher for a free item or a reduction of a set amount handed to the first 50 customers to enter the shop – could provide useful advertising and goodwill (except from customer number 51!).

Do not overlook the value of giving a personal welcome to those first customers as they enter the door. Putting the human touch to a business enterprise, if done well and sincerely, can only be of value to the business.

Remember this: Wangle free publicity

Find out from your local paper when they are likely to run special promotional sections like wedding fayres (they seem to like that spelling), DIY, health and beauty or gardening features. As a new shop you might be able to wangle an editorial; the advertising space will usually be cheaper as well.

Try it now: Plan your marketing strategy

You may well have written your marketing strategy when you were making your business plan, particularly if you needed start-up capital. Apply this now to the opening of your shop. Design posters, flyers, leaflets, etc., all matching your image, with your name and logo. Remember to include where you are and any opening day incentives. As they say, 'It pays to advertise'.

Focus points

✲ Be very clear about your customers and what they are most likely to buy, with a good stock balance.

✲ Decide early on what your image is and create advertising material to enhance that image. Remember the security aspects of your shop and make sure you know the law as it applies to you.

✲ Above all, be excited about your shop and give it 100 per cent of your time, energy and flair.

✲ And good luck!

Next step

You may well be combining the opening of your shop with running a home, so Chapter 11 is concerned with you and your home circumstances. How much planning are you able to do? What about children and other dependants? And how about you, yourself – can you really run a business and your home, with the help and support of those at home? You will certainly need it.

Running a home and a business

In this chapter you will learn:

▶ *About managing the tricky balance between your home and professional life*

▶ *How to involve the whole family in looking after the home*

▶ *How to make sure your dependants – young children, elderly relatives and others – are well cared for during your absence, leaving you free from worry and guilt*

▶ *How to look after your own health, through regular medical check-ups and sensible diet and fitness regimes.*

Starting your own business is hard work, and takes a lot of time and energy. Unless the domestic side of your life is organized, you will find it very difficult to give the business the concentration it needs. If you get to work worrying about the gardening or the ironing which did not get done, you will find it difficult to give your whole attention to your business matters. You need to be either the sort of person who does not mind living in chaos at home – and whose family does not mind living in chaos either – or the sort of person who is well organized.

Self-assessment: Think about your work life/home life balance

1 What sort of plans do you need to make to marry your business and your home?

2 What is the current division of labour in your household?

3 What sort of domestic help do you have?

4 What dependants do you have?

5 How healthy are you and other members of your household?

6 What sort of food do you eat?

7 What exercise do you get?

8 How business-like do you appear to others?

9 How flexible are you?

10 How many hours a week can you devote to your business without detriment to your home life?

We all have our own way of organizing our domestic life, so this chapter does not say that you should or should not do certain things. It tries to give you some ideas which will help you to organize yourself and your family to include the extra business dimension. Whether you are a man or a woman, you very probably have domestic responsibilities, but you may need to reallocate these to accommodate your new business.

Planning ahead

No matter how much other people in the household help, it is still very important to plan the routine, which includes either shopping or, at the very least, making a shopping list.

If you have been used to shopping frequently – perhaps a little every day or so – you will need to think about shopping less often, so that it is not so time-consuming. If you run a freezer efficiently, you do not need to shop more often than once a week, providing you plan ahead. Some people do a 'bake-in' for the whole week ahead as well. Internet shopping can be a great help, but you need to make delivery arrangements.

It is useful to keep a note in your diary of what everyone else is doing, as well as your own business engagements, and a family diary or wall chart is sensible. If you can persuade members of the household to declare what they are going to be doing at least a week ahead, and put it down in the family diary, it helps you to plan who needs to eat what, and when. Try not to keep too many diaries (one personal one and one family should be enough) or you will find it difficult to keep them up to date.

You will also need to plan ahead for such things as:

▶ children's activities

▶ business dinners

▶ family holidays and breaks

▶ visits to the vet (if you have pets)

▶ visits from service engineers etc.

▶ clothes shopping

▶ social and leisure activities.

It may sound a bit regimented if you are not used to planning your life in this way, but if you like to live an organized sort of life, you will find that careful planning is essential to your peace of mind and the success of your business. It also gives the family a sense of security, although you have to guard against a lack of flexibility: always having smoked mackerel salad on a Friday starts as a joke, but can finally become an irritant.

Remember this: Make your electronic diaries accessible

If all diaries are electronic, make sure everyone who needs to can access the others. Alternatively, keep a paper desk diary.

Division of labour

If you are to run your business successfully, you really do need the support of the people at home, not just occasionally, but all the time. It is illogical for people to sit around waiting for you to get home to get the evening meal: perhaps a 'first in starts the meal' routine would work for your household.

Each family will have its own way of sorting out who does what. But it is important that everyone, including the smallest of the children, does something on a regular basis. Three-year-olds can tidy their toys away; five-year-olds can dust; ten-year-olds can help prepare vegetables; fourteen-year-olds can cope with washing, ironing and cooking. Everyone can help with the washing up and the cleaning. Discuss these things with the family, and see who can do what, and how they can best fit it in with their own timetable. Obviously, only adults can drive cars, but almost everyone can push a vacuum-cleaner around.

In some households the chores seem to fall naturally into traditional male and female jobs; in others, who does what is by preference. Women often find that only they are prepared to clean the lavatory and the bath. You can encourage everyone in the family to look after their personal belongings, which means both male and female cleaning their shoes – again there is no logical reason why they should not.

In a busy household the garden often gets neglected. If you are a tidy person, this will niggle away at the back of your mind, particularly if you care what the neighbours say – and many people do. It is helpful to have a garden which is easy to cope with, and which other family members do not mind working in. Go for easily kept lawns and shrubs, or patios. Plenty of ground cover keeps the weeds at bay. No garden will look reasonable if left totally unattended – even if your garden is a window box, the plants still need watering – but you can make it easier for yourself and other members of the household if you plan the garden carefully and agree with the others on who will do what. Gardening can be a very good way of getting away from the business for a while, and you will need to do that from time to time.

Case study

A married couple with children decided that, as well as employing someone to help in the house, they would employ someone to help in the garden. The problem was that, as well as having to clear up the house for the cleaner, they also had to clear up the garden for the gardener!

USING HELP

Some people manage to do everything superbly well: they run a business, a house and a social life, and have really good relationships with people at home and at work, and you wonder how they do it.

One of the secrets often is that they use all the help they can get, both human and mechanical. Reliable help with the cleaning, washing and ironing is not easy to find, but if you can find someone at least to do the heavy cleaning, it is well worth the expense. You need not feel guilty or inadequate because you are paying someone else to do what perhaps you consider is your responsibility. You are earning money elsewhere, and you cannot do everything yourself; employing someone to help in the home or the garden benefits you and the person you are employing to do the job. It may take time to find the right person, but it is worth persevering. Using help is a strength, not a weakness.

You should also use all the mechanical help you can get, such as a really efficient washing machine and dryer, a dishwasher and a microwave, if you like that method of cooking. Use appliances which make your life, and that of everyone else in the household, easier. This might mean updating your appliances more frequently than you are used to doing. It is normally worth the money and the effort.

Try it now: Who does what?

This exercise does not set out to test you on your ability to plan and organize your domestic life, but to help you decide where you need to make changes so that running a business and a home can work for you and other members of the household. Some sections may not apply to your circumstances.

Copy out or otherwise reproduce the table below. Under 'Changes needed' write what precisely you need to change and how you are going to do it. Put a tick where everything is OK.

	All OK	Who	Changes needed
Diaries			
Shopping			
Washing			
Ironing			
Cleaning			
The garden			
Domestic appliances			
Childcare			
Other dependants			

TIME AND PEOPLE

Your business will find it more difficult to thrive if your domestic background is unstable. This means making time to be with your home partner and the children, if you have any. You might have to work some evenings and weekends, but if you make it every evening and weekend, undercurrents of dissatisfaction are likely to start up at home, and you will lose the goodwill and support of the people you need most.

Children need a stable home base, and they need to know that their parents have the time and the interest to care about their activities and their worries. This is common sense, of course, but it is amazing how easy it is to get caught up in the excitement and freedom of doing your own thing, and to forget, very gradually, how much you are needed and wanted at home. It is a fine balance to strike but, if sensitively handled, need not mean that either home or business has to suffer.

Children and other dependants

You might be the type of person who feels guilty at letting other people look after the children or other dependants – an elderly relative, perhaps. Very few people – especially women – escape this sense of guilt at some time or other, particularly when they leave a new baby in the care of others for the first time. Other members of the family, perhaps your own parents, can often make you feel guilty as well, sometimes quite deliberately.

One way of coping with this is to acknowledge the sense of guilt, and then do everything that you can to make sure that your children and other dependants are well cared for when you are not with them. This part of Chapter 11 will concentrate on caring for children. In all cases make sure that those who care for your children are CRB checked.

TYPES OF PAID CHILDCARE

▶ **Nannies**

Nannies look after children in your own home. This can be as a live-in nanny, a daily nanny, or one who lives in during the week and goes home at weekends.

Some nannies have been to top-class training establishments, and are fully qualified in all aspects of childcare. The training is thorough and expensive. A qualified nanny will be seeking a well-paid position, often as a live-in nanny, with excellent domestic facilities, working conditions and hours. These are often the nannies who answer advertisements in *The Lady*, which seems to be the leading 'top nanny' recruitment medium, if one can put it that way. These nannies will have excellent references, and can be relied upon to do a thoroughly competent and reliable job, combined with real care for the children, in a suitable household.

If you are looking for a less highly qualified nanny, who perhaps will look after your children on a daily basis (some hours or days with you, some with another family), look in local nanny agencies, Job Centres and advertisements in the local paper. You can advertise in the local paper yourself, of course.

Agencies do not necessarily 'screen' the applicants for your particular job – some do and some do not. You usually have to pay a registration fee as an employer and the agency will send you prospective nannies for you to interview. You need to find out from the agency what you are paying for – it might be just the introduction, or the agency might do a certain amount of selection on your behalf. They will need to know how much you are prepared to pay (usually by the hour); an agency or a Job Centre can advise you on this.

What are you looking for in a nanny? Obviously someone who likes, and can deal with, children. When you interview a prospective nanny, make sure it is at a time when your children are around and awake. Let the nanny play with them or hold them, and watch the reactions of the nanny and the children.

It is also important that the nanny's personality is compatible with yours. If you have a fairly strong personality (and you have to be able to acknowledge this), a nanny with an equally forceful outlook on life could cause problems. On the other hand, you do not want anyone who is not capable of following instructions and taking decisions when necessary. There can be clashes of culture as well as personality; young nannies sometimes move from one part of the country to another, or from one country to another, and their diet and background could be quite different from yours and what you want for your children. This need not be a problem if you are clear about what you want, and if you are both prepared to be understanding and a little flexible. It is something to consider when engaging a nanny to look after your children.

A nanny will expect to do everything connected with the children, according to the hours of work agreed. At the start you will need to make lists of the children's routines, roughly what you would like them to eat for their meals, and what you want them to wear, and so on. A nanny will not expect to do the housework, except where it is directly connected with the children – their clothes, their meals. Unless you have fairly well-delineated areas of work, there can be conflict between a nanny and, say, the person who does the cleaning in the house: the one could resent what the other does and does not do. Incidentally, cleaners and home helps often get paid rather more than nannies.

▶ Mother's or father's help

A mother's or father's help is someone (usually a woman) who is prepared to do a bit of everything – looking after the children and some domestic work. These women are often not professionally qualified, but are quite capable of looking after children and doing some of the domestic chores, such as light cleaning, washing and ironing. They would expect to be paid more than just a nanny or just a cleaner, but could be less expensive than employing both.

You will find mother's or father's helps through agencies, Job Centres and advertisements in the local press. You both (employer and employed) need to be clear about what you expect, what the job entails and what the payment is going to be. A mother's or father's help is also someone who is going to look after your children, so you need to be just as careful about selection as if you were employing a nanny.

▶ Au pairs

These are (usually) young women from abroad whose main aim is to live in the UK for a while to improve their English. They will normally want to live in with the family, so need reasonable living accommodation and time off. They will probably be happy to do light housework as well as look after the children.

Because an au pair is usually a young person, you will have a certain amount of responsibility for her welfare in this country, and you will probably be required to allow her specific time off to pursue her English studies.

It is helpful to employ au pairs through agencies who specialize in this area of work because they can advise you on your responsibilities as well as what you can expect from an au pair. An au pair will not expect to be paid a great deal of money, but she will expect to live and be treated as part of the family.

▶ Childminders

If your business allows you to work regular hours and you can be sure to deliver and collect your children, a registered childminder can be a good way of making sure your children are well cared for. Childminders often have children of their own at home, and are happy to add to their family on a regular basis and look after other people's children as well as their own.

Childminders have to be registered with the local authority because their facilities, safety and competence are monitored. Lists of registered childminders can be obtained from the Social Services department of your local authority. Many childminders are prepared to look after your children for long hours, or for odd hours, provided it is on a regular basis.

ILLNESS AND HOLIDAYS

It is when your children are ill that you are likely to feel most torn between your business and your family. Perhaps you have an important client to meet, and a phone call comes through that your child is ill. What do you do? Perhaps your instincts are to rush home and let the client know that the meeting will have to be postponed. On the other hand, you are in business, and if you have not got a business partner who can cover for you, perhaps your domestic partner, or another member of the family, can cope with the immediate problem, and you can take it from there. Make all necessary arrangements, and try to put the illness out of your mind until you have completed your business, unless of course it is very serious. Then you can drop everything else and give your child all your attention.

Holidays are another matter and can be planned for. Some local authorities provide facilities for looking after children too young to be left on their own during school holidays and half terms. One of the benefits of being self-employed is that you can sometimes arrange your workload round school holidays, depending on the nature of the business and the people with whom you work.

If you have to leave young teenagers on their own during the day, they sometimes find it acceptable for you to leave, every morning, a plan of action for the day, which can include jobs to do and, perhaps, outings or activities that you have prearranged or for which you have bought a ticket. It takes quite a lot of thought and organization on your part, but can be useful for only children, or children whose friends have all decided to be away at the same time.

Holidays do not just take care of themselves. Again, it helps to plan fairly carefully, but allow some flexibility.

OTHER DEPENDANTS

It depends whether other people who are dependent on you are living in your house or on their own. In either case, if they have been used to having you around, it is going to be difficult for both parties to accept that some of your time is going to be allocated elsewhere. You may face accusations that you are unfeeling and ambitious, which, again, will make you feel guilty.

As with children, provided you have made every provision possible for the care and welfare of dependent relatives (home helps, local shopping services, meals on wheels), there is no reason why you should not go about your business with a clear mind. Enlist the help of other members of your family, including your own children and your domestic partner, and remember your own brothers and sisters.

Involve dependants in the decisions which have to be made, and share with them as far as possible the excitement – and the worries – of running your own business. It could add an extra dimension to their lives.

> **Try it now: Make a care to-do list**
>
> ✳ If you have children and/or other dependants, make a to-do list of all the things you need to find out and decide for their care.
> ✳ If you have pets, how will you manage their care?

Your health

When you are self-employed you cannot afford to be ill, and you usually have not got the time to be ill. Certainly, a busy life and being really interested in what you are doing makes you less inclined to have or notice minor ailments.

As far as major illnesses are concerned, you need to do all you can to prevent these. Your lifestyle and regular medical check-ups will make sure you are healthy and fit to maintain the energy and stamina which you will certainly need.

YOUR LIFESTYLE

When you are very busy, you are tempted not to eat properly.
Stress and digestive disorders can build up if you never have
breakfast, do not stop for lunch, rush home and get the evening
meal and then eat it in a hurry. If you can discipline yourself
to have a definite break for lunch, even if it is only a short one,
your productivity will remain high in the afternoon.

Sometimes you can get caught up in a lot of business lunches;
too many of those can ruin your figure as well as your digestion.
However, it is acceptable to be seen not to eat too much at
lunchtime and not to drink too much. In fact, women have an
advantage here, because they do not have to project a macho
image. You can easily drift into high alcohol consumption, but
fortunately it is now quite all right to be seen not to drink if
you are driving, or to have a mineral water with your lunch or
dinner wine.

It goes without saying, and this is common sense, that a well-
balanced diet is what you need to keep healthy. The problem is
that you can get so busy trying to run at least two lives at once
that you ignore this aspect of your lifestyle, and eat and drink
too much or too little.

It is not easy to fit in regular exercise because often you cannot
stick to a very strict timetable. But if you can swim, walk, do
keep fit, play tennis, squash or football or do something in the
way of exercise on a regular basis, it will certainly help to keep
your body trim and, of course, your clothes will look better on
you. At the very least, walk up stairs instead of taking lifts, do
not ride where you can walk and try to get a little exercise in
every day.

Some people seem to survive on very little sleep, and some
people need a lot. Whatever your necessary quota, try to make
sure that you get it. If someone is ill, you cannot, perhaps,
help staying up all night, but it does not do you any good to
lie awake worrying – the problem will not be solved, and your
body and mind will not be refreshed. Try to finish all you
have to do before you go to bed, and be determined to leave
everything else until the next day. Some people can catnap
during the day, and find this refreshing; if you are that type of

person, it can be better to stop off at a motorway service station for 15 minutes and have a sleep, rather than arrive feeling worn out. If you decide to sleep in your car, remember to shut all windows and lock all doors for safety's sake, and park in the middle of the car park rather than in a quiet corner.

If you are able to fit it in, it is a good idea to spend some time each week doing something which has nothing to do with work, and nothing to do with home. Regular exercise can be one such activity, but joining a group to share interests or learn something new can be equally relaxing and therapeutic. You need a little time for yourself.

PREVENTIVE MEDICINE

If you are self-employed, you cannot claim sickness benefit from an employer or from the state. Some people take out insurance cover for lost earnings if they are sick, as well as covering the cost of treatment to enable them to get back to work as quickly as possible.

Another form of insurance is to have a full, regular medical check-up, probably annually. These are given at well woman, or well man clinics, which are sometimes available on the National Health, or privately. A regular check-up means that any illness can be detected at an early stage, and the cure is often swift and complete – less time away from your business. Women should take advantage of breast screening and cervical smear testing, particularly if they are in high-risk age groups.

As well as detecting the early signs of disease, a doctor giving you regular check-ups can also advise you on your general health. It is obvious to you if you are putting on or losing too much weight, but high blood pressure or a high cholesterol level is not obvious. These are checked in a full medical, and your doctor will advise you on diet and exercise.

Addiction to smoking or drugs of any sort, including tranquillizers, will damage your health. If you know you take too many pills, or cannot stop smoking, seek help. You cannot afford to let such things drain away your energies. If as a woman you know you suffer from PMT or 'disabling' periods, go to your doctor. There are often things which can be done to alleviate discomfort, and you might as well take the trouble to sort these things out, rather than put up with it every month.

Your health is very precious, and you need to be in good health to run a business successfully. Look after it.

Try it now: Keep a food and fitness diary

✱ Make a diary of what you eat, everything at every meal, for a week. If you are not eating a balanced diet or are not eating regularly, decide what needs changing and change it.

✱ Do the same for daily exercise.

✱ Starting a new business is a good time for making other, often quite small, changes in your lifestyle.

Remember this: Get a gym buddy

Exercising with a friend (running or going to the gym, for example) can be more fun than doing it on your own.

Your business image

You are in business, and need to look, sound and appear business-like. This means that your whole image should reflect you and the type of business you run. It does not mean that women have to give up their femininity, but nor should they exploit it.

YOUR APPEARANCE

Try to choose a style of dress and hairstyle which suits you and the image you want to project. This does not necessarily mean that you need to keep up with every latest fashion, unless you are in that type of business yourself. It does mean that you need to keep your wardrobe reasonably up to date in both style and colour.

It can be a good idea to buy several items which you can mix and match, having chosen your colour scheme for the season or the year. There are many businesses who can advise you on the sort of style and colouring which is the best for you and your particular image. If you are the sort of person who finds it difficult to decide on what is best for you, a visit to that type of establishment could be a worthwhile investment. You can find their advertisements in professional and business magazines and publications, and they usually cater for both men and women.

If your wardrobe has been geared to a home environment, you will need to take time to plan and build up a business wardrobe gradually. Your hair needs to be easy to look after, and yet look smart and stylish, without being way out. For a woman, a style which can be washed frequently and dried with ease is a great asset – and so is an efficient hairdryer.

Again, for a woman, it is important to be strict about not driving in business shoes – nothing ruins the heels more quickly. It is worth having a pair of driving shoes which you keep in the car and which you can slip on and off easily. Keep a spare pair of knee-highs or stockings in your briefcase.

Bags and briefcases say a lot about you. If your bag or briefcase is in a muddle, you will project a 'muddly' image. A slim briefcase, containing only the papers you need for that day, shows an orderly mind, and therefore an orderly way of doing business. If your bag or briefcase is of good quality, it will last longer and project a quality image of you. Buy as good as you can afford. It does not enhance your image to arrive with an overflowing, cheap bag and a plastic carrier bag! A laptop carrier looks much better.

Your car is part of your image, too. It does not matter if it is small and elderly, provided it is well cared for and clean. A car full of children's bits and pieces is not a good idea; try to leave those at home.

Try it now: Assess your dress

If you have the courage, imagine you are going to your first business meeting or your first networking group. Dress from top to toe in what you think you will wear, including makeup if appropriate. Then complete the look with your handbag and/or briefcase. Now look at yourself critically in a mirror, or ask your partner or a friend to tell you what image you portray. It could be quite revealing.

YOUR SOCIAL SKILLS

When greeting anyone for the first time, shake hands, firmly; do the same when saying goodbye. It helps to break down the initial barrier between you and to end a meeting on a friendly note. Most meetings, whether they are large, formal meetings or small, informal ones, usually start off with some small talk between you and your customer or client. Stick to neutral topics like the weather, the journey or the car park. People do not want to talk, at that stage, about burning issues of the day, or about domestic topics. However, it is useful to keep up to date with what is going on in current affairs, the business world and/or sport, so that you can talk with a reasonable amount of knowledge about these things, if the occasion arises.

Accept offers of tea, coffee or other refreshments, and be definite about how you like each. Changing your mind about such apparently trivial matters at the start of a business acquaintance or meeting is not a good beginning.

Some men still regard businesswomen with suspicion. They can feel superior, or threatened, or both. If you are a woman in business treat men with quiet confidence, showing that you know your business but have no wish to be over-friendly, and you should not have any problems. Some men are quite happy to do business with women, but still like to treat them as women in such matters as opening doors, carrying heavy loads and so on. Do not expect men to do this, but if they wish to do so, accept graciously. It makes them feel good and will not diminish your standing in any way.

Remember that some decisions are made in the men's or women's toilets; be aware of several men or women disappearing at the same time and returning with a united front. If you are aware of such things, you can counteract them if necessary.

It is worthwhile learning about food and wines, if you do not already know these things, so that you can handle situations in bars and restaurants with confidence and ease. You do not have to be over-assertive, but you can make your position known with calm authority, and you should do so.

As a person starting out in business you need to earn the respect of other businesspeople in all sorts of situations.

Remember this: First impressions count

You never get a second chance to make a first impression.

Case study: Health and wealth

A single businesswoman in her fifties decided she was overweight, drank too much and was too stressed out. What did she do? She committed herself, in writing, to someone she could trust. She 'promised' to return to Weight Watchers, start running again and concentrate on the more enjoyable and profitable parts of her business. So what happened? After about three months and something of struggle, she lost weight, drank less, went running with a friend who wanted to learn from her (great for her ego) and cut out those parts of her business which were really causing her grief. The trusted friend encouraged her all along the way and the result is a healthier, happier, more prosperous businesswoman.

Focus points

✳ Balancing home and work is never easy, but as a self-employed person you do have some control over how you achieve this.

✳ Good planning is one of the great secrets to the success of making sure the home runs smoothly and that dependent relatives (and pets) are properly cared for.

✳ Looking after your own health and lifestyle is crucial, too.

Next, and last, steps

The final chapter in this book deals with the professionals: what they can do for you and how to find them; managing contractors and subcontractors; and where to go for help and information. You are bound to need some of this at some time, so Chapter 12 is an easy reference source.

The professionals

This chapter contains:

▶ *Information about the various professionals who can help you with your small business, such as accountants and business clubs*

▶ *Templates for you to use or copy for your personal directory of the people who can help you*

▶ *Information about managing subcontractors*

▶ *Useful website addresses.*

Your personal directory

ACCOUNTANTS

An accountant's expertise lies mainly in the following areas:

▶ end-of-year accounts

▶ submission to appropriate authorities

▶ tax returns

▶ advice on what can and cannot be claimed for tax purposes

▶ all matters concerned with income and expenditure

▶ business plans

▶ cash flow forecasts

▶ HM Revenue & Customs

Name of company:

Address:

Contact name:

Telephone number:

Mobile number:

Email address:

Website:

NOTES:

BANKS AND BUILDING SOCIETIES

Main areas of expertise:

- ▶ business bank account
- ▶ overdraft facilities
- ▶ standing orders
- ▶ loans
- ▶ advice on business plans
- ▶ advice on cash flow forecasts
- ▶ money transfers
- ▶ mortgages
- ▶ import transactions

Name of bank or building society:

Address:

Contact name:

Telephone number:

Mobile number:

Email address:

Website:

NOTES:

BOOK-KEEPERS

Areas of expertise:

▶ doing the books

▶ invoicing

▶ banking

▶ petty cash

▶ wages and salaries

▶ VAT returns

▶ income and expenditure account

Name of company:

Address:

Contact name:

Telephone number:

Mobile number:

Email address:

Website:

NOTES:

BUSINESS CLUBS

Opportunities:

▶ networking

▶ support

▶ promotional literature

▶ newsletters

▶ local contacts

Name of club:

Address:

Contact name:

Telephone number:

Mobile number:

Email address:

Website:

NOTES:

CHAMBER OF COMMERCE

Opportunities:

▶ networking

▶ wide range of businesses

▶ local expertise

▶ well known locally

Name of local Chamber:

Address:

Contact name:

Telephone number:

Mobile number:

Email address:

Website:

NOTES:

ESTATE AGENTS

Areas of expertise:

- ► selling and buying property
- ► renting premises
- ► advice on surveys
- ► inventories

Name of company:

Address:

Contact name:

Telephone number:

Mobile number:

Email address:

Website:

NOTES:

INSURANCE BROKERS

Areas of expertise: all types of insurance, including:

- ▶ vehicles
- ▶ business premises and contents
- ▶ public liability
- ▶ personal accident
- ▶ loss of earnings
- ▶ professional indemnity
- ▶ life

Name of company:

Address:

Contact name:

Telephone number:

Mobile number:

Email address:

Website:

NOTES:

PC SUPPLIERS

Areas of expertise: suppliers of advice, hardware and software, including:

- ▶ laptops
- ▶ PCs
- ▶ photocopiers
- ▶ printers
- ▶ fax machines
- ▶ cables
- ▶ speakers

Name of company:

Address:

Contact name:

Telephone number:

Mobile number:

Email address:

Website:

NOTES:

SECRETARIAL SERVICES

Areas of expertise:

▶ writing letters, emails, reports, proposals

▶ keying in and printing out

▶ proofreading

▶ dealing with incoming mail and email

▶ telephone work

Name of company:

Address:

Contact name:

Telephone number:

Mobile number:

Email address:

Website:

NOTES:

SOLICITORS

Areas of expertise:

► Memorandum and Articles of Association

► Partnership Agreement

► leases and rental agreements

► contracts

► employment law

► Data Protection Act

Name of company:

Address:

Contact name:

Telephone number:

Mobile number:

Email address:

Website:

NOTES:

WEBSITE DESIGNERS AND MANAGERS

Areas of expertise:

- ▶ website design
- ▶ software advice
- ▶ website maintenance and updating
- ▶ Internet service provider
- ▶ analysis of website visits

Name of company:

Address:

Contact name:

Telephone number:

Mobile number:

Email address:

Website:

NOTES:

Managing subcontractors

A bad subcontractor or associate can really ruin your reputation for good customer service. The same can be said for people you recommend, although you have less control over them. Associates and subcontractors can be managed, however, and should be managed so that the customer's whole experience is good. Businesspeople such as accountants, trainers or consultants often have a network of associates they can call on if they cannot undertake the work themselves. Businesspeople such as builders and manufacturers often need to use subcontractors.

Take a builder as an example: there are builders who work on building sites and those who work in people's homes. Both will need to use a variety of scaffolding erectors, bricklayers, carpenters, electricians, plumbers and heating engineers – a lot of tradespeople to co-ordinate and manage. This section will concentrate on builders who work in people's homes, but the procedures for managing their subcontractors will apply, in general, to almost anyone who employs subcontractors or associates.

HOW DO YOU FIND THEM?
Usually by reputation and word of mouth is best. Where you can, avoid using those whose adverts constantly appear in local papers or *Yellow Pages* or *Thomson Local* – you wonder why they have to do so much advertising, although some might be suitable. Subcontractors who work on building sites are also best avoided because they have different work routines and are likely to be less flexible in their hours of work. In addition, they may not be used to dealing directly with customers.

If you are a builder, new to a district, and looking for good subcontractors, drive around and see where other builders, probably with subcontractors, are working in people's homes. When the builder has gone home for the day, ring the bell and ask the customers what they think of the builder and anyone else working on that job; they are usually happy to tell you. Customer feedback can work for manufacturers and consultants, too. If you are starting up your business in a small town or village, do some networking. Because it is a small place, someone is always bound to know the best tradespeople by reputation.

HOW DO YOU KNOW THEIR STANDARDS?

Customer service depends on good standards from everyone, not only work standards, but social skills as well. Having chosen your subcontractor, take them round to the customer and introduce them. The reason for this is threefold:

1 The subcontractor can see the size of the job.

2 The customer can begin to build a relationship with the subcontractor, as well as with you.

3 You can listen and watch to see how the subcontractor conducts himself (or occasionally herself) in a person's home, how he speaks to the customer and how well he explains his part of the project.

Once the project is underway, you must monitor their standards, by turning up every now and again if you happen to be working elsewhere for a while. If you are working together, you set your own high standards of workmanship and conduct, so your subcontractors should follow suit. Just a small thing like taking off muddy boots before you go into the house, or asking if you can move something, will be noticed and appreciated by the customer. In other words, lead by example.

WHAT SORT OF AGREEMENT?

Do you have a verbal agreement with a subcontractor or a written one? If you have been working together for some time and the job is fairly straightforward, such as a subcontractor coming to fell one tree which is too near the house, the agreement as to the extent of the job and what you are going to pay can probably be verbal. If you do not know the subcontractor well (perhaps it is the first time you have worked together), and particularly if it is a large, complicated project, a written agreement is better. You might even have to get it drawn up by a solicitor. With a written agreement you each know the extent of the work, the planned timescale and the payment and settlement terms. Check that the subcontractors have their insurances in place. You, yourself, will usually have public liability insurance, in case the customer is harmed or the property damaged, and your personal accident insurance. Subcontractors should also have personal accident insurance to cover their particular trade. You should also have employers' liability insurance for the time you employ a subcontractor.

HOW DO YOU BUILD, AND KEEP, GOOD RELATIONSHIPS WITH SUBCONTRACTORS?

Pay them on time! Even if you are waiting for your money, you should pay the subcontractors as agreed. Some large companies make the subcontractor wait until they, themselves, have been paid, which is not good practice for a builder running a small business, perhaps on their own. Subcontractors are your customers, so will look for reliability from you: turning up on time, arranging for materials to be delivered and all the things that help the job go smoothly.

In addition, good communication is vital. Keep your subcontractor informed of every little detail about what is going on. Perhaps customers change their minds in the middle of a project – they prefer the power socket to be at waist level instead of on the skirting board. They tell you, but if you fail to pass it on to the electrician in good time, the socket will be in the wrong place. Tea and lunch breaks offer a good opportunity to chat, banter and build relationships and to exchange information about the job.

You hope your subcontractors are as reliable as you, but it is as well to contact them a short time before you start a project to check they have not forgotten. After all, the project may have been agreed many months ago. At the same time you can confirm what time you are planning to be there – perhaps the customer does not want you to arrive until after nine in the morning, after the school run.

WHAT IF A CUSTOMER COMPLAINS?

You sort it out. It is up to you to do this as quickly as possible. Establish the exact cause for the complaint. Was it shoddy workmanship, tools left lying around where people could fall over them, subcontractors not turning up on time, or continually going off early without letting the customer know, perhaps just lack of thought and common courtesy? Whatever it is, you have to put the matter right and leave the customer happy.

If you find the subcontractor was at fault, you must let them know – mistakes can be made – not necessarily over the phone that same evening, but perhaps at the start of work the next day. Also, if a customer complains directly to the subcontractor, encourage them to pass the complaint on to you, however small it is. You need to know when things go wrong. You must be able to trust each other and be honest with each other. Your reputation is on the line and as a builder in a small way of business, your reputation for excellent customer service is one of the most valuable things you have.

If you employ subcontractors of any sort, this checklist will be helpful to you. You should be able to answer 'yes' to every appropriate item. Have you:

▶ found a suitable subcontractor?

▶ introduced him or her to the customer or client?

▶ agreed the job specification?

▶ agreed payment and settlement terms?

▶ drawn up a written contract, if necessary?

▶ checked the subcontractor's insurances?

▶ agreed date and start time for the project?

▶ checked that the subcontractor is going to turn up?

▶ monitored the subcontractor's standards?

▶ passed on all necessary information in detail?

▶ helped out where necessary?

- dealt with any customer complaints?
- passed them on to the subcontractor?
- made sure everything is finished and cleared away?
- paid your subcontractor promptly?

For the time a subcontractor is working for you, you are employing him or her. Remember that special tax rules apply to subcontractors in the construction industry.

Useful website addresses

ACAS

Employment relations www.acas.org.uk

Advertising

Yellow Pages www.yell.com

Thomson www.thomsonlocal.com

Advice

Business information (formerly Business Link) www.gov.uk

Enterprise First www.enterprisefirst.co.uk

Federation of Small Businesses www.fsb.org.uk

A new business

Business names, trademarks, etc. www.anewbusiness.co.uk

Charities: HM Revenue & Customs Charities

The Charity Commission www.charity-commission.gov.uk

Helpsheets https://www.gov.uk/government/publications/charities-detailed-guidance-notes

Tax reliefs and obligations www.hmrc.gov.uk/charities/index.htm

Equality and Human Rights Commission www.equalityhumanrights.com

Companies Registration Office www.companieshouse.gov.uk

Data Protection www.ico.gov.uk

Department for Business Innovation & Skills www.bis.gov.uk

Department of Work and Pensions www.dwp.gov.uk

Employment rights

Public services information: www.gov.uk

Equality and Human Rights Commission
www.equalityhumanrights.com

Europe

Entrepreneural Inspiration www.enspire.eu

European Information Service Centre www.eiscltd.eu

Export

The Institute of Export www.export.org.uk

UK Trade and Investment www.ukti.gov.uk

Simplifying International Trade www.gov.uk

Franchising

British Franchise Association www.thebfa.org.uk

Health and Safety Executive www.hse.gov.uk

Intellectual property

UK Intellectual Property Office www.ipo.gov.uk

Marketing

The Chartered Institute of Marketing www.cim.co.uk

Pensions

The Pensions Regulator www.thepensionsregulator.gov.uk

Taxation and VAT

HM Revenue & Customs www.hmrc.gov.uk

Answers to 'Employing others' quiz (Chapter 9)

1 **True:** Listing the 'essentials' and 'desirables' helps with a first sift.

2 **False:** A job description is a much fuller description of the entire role, and may include a schedule of duties.

3 **False:** Which is why you must be careful what you write.

4 **True:** There are different regulations for older children.

5 **False:** People may work to any age.

6 **False:** Religion or belief and age have been left out.

7 **True:** An employer must also deduct employees' National Insurance contributions.

8 **True:** Also P60s and P45s, if appropriate.

9 **False:** Sick pay is not necessary for the first three working days.

10 **True:** There are also other payments which can be claimed back.

11 **False:** Only after they have worked for the company for over 26 weeks.

12 **True:** But for five employees or over, they must introduce the government's pension arrangements.

13 **False:** Part-time workers are entitled only to 28 days' pro rata holiday.

14 **True:** This must be done within two months of an employee starting a job.

15 **False:** Incompetence is a ground for dismissal, but the disciplinary procedure must be followed.

16 **False:** Staff employed for less than one week are not entitled to notice of dismissal.

17 **False:** Everyone in business, employers, the self-employed and employees all have a duty of care under HASAWA.

18 **True:** An employee has a right to see the data and correct it if necessary.

Index